Second Edition

Observing Ourselves

Essays in Social Research

Earl Babbie
Chapman University

WAVELAND

PRESS, INC.

Long Grove, Illinois

For information about this book, contact:
Waveland Press, Inc.
4180 IL Route 83, Suite 101
Long Grove, IL 60047-9580
(847) 634-0081
info@waveland.com
www.waveland.com

In memory of
Annie Woolcutt

Contents

Preface

Is social science possible? This is a question well worth asking, since there is no doubt that social research will be conducted and is being conducted right now. The question I want to raise is whether we can observe ourselves *scientifically*. Is it possible for human beings to study other human beings (not to mention themselves) as scientifically as physicists study inorganic matter and force or as scientifically as microbiologists study cells and tissue? This question has vitally concerned the practitioners of sociology, psychology, anthropology, economics, political science, and allied fields for more than a century and a half. The same question should be of more than passing interest to the rest of humanity.

Rocks and cells do not study themselves or each other, though human beings study them. And although whales and porpoises may be as intelligent as human beings there is no evidence that they study us scientifically. Science seems a uniquely human activity. So who is better qualified to study human beings than you and me?

This book addresses a number of the fundamental philosophical and methodological issues involved in the scientific study of human beings. As one who has devoted a career to social research, I make no bones that I believe good social science is both possible and vital, yet I feel it is important to guard against a social science that merely attempts to mimic a misunderstood image of the natural sciences.

If we are to study human beings in a way that enhances what it means to be human, we should not simply attempt to create a "social physics," as Auguste Comte and other initially envisioned early in the nineteenth century. Rather, we must create a science that is in many ways more sophisticated and ultimately more powerful than any science yet realized or conceived.

It is my intention that the issues raised in this little book will engage you and help you discover what it takes for human beings to study human beings. My plan is that you and I will discover those things together.

A book such as this does not spring full-grown from a head of cabbage. Many people have contributed importantly to it. Those teachers, colleagues, and students who have influenced the ideas expressed in this book are by now so numerous that I cannot possibly acknowledge them all by name. Instead, as a way of acknowledging the kind of people who have given their ideas to you through this book, I request that you perform one act today on behalf of all the residents of this planet.

More immediately, some colleagues have contributed specifically to this volume. Ted Wagenaar, Miami University; Kathleen McKinney, Illinois State University; and Gary Cretser, Cal State Poly at Pomona were kind enough to review the manuscript and offer useful suggestions for improving it.

Thanks to everyone at Waveland Press who made this second edition possible, particularly Gayle Zawilla, my editor, and Katy Murphy, my typesetter. Their dedication and attention to detail made the transition from *manuscript* to *book* seamless and easy.

Finally, I have dedicated this book to Annie Woolcutt, who, as I describe in the reflexive introduction, helped launch my career in social research. The last time I talked to her, she was under siege by cancer. After dedicating her life to helping others, she was finally helpless, locked in pain. Her last words to me were of her late husband. "Why doesn't Basil come to get me? I can't understand it. Do you know why he doesn't come for me?" I couldn't give an answer, but on July 4, 1985, Basil came and set Annie free. Now, she lives for me as the lady who voted for Gene Autry, early and often.

Reflexive Introduction

You are holding in your hands a book of essays in the field of social science research. Though not intended as a textbook, it can be used as a supplementary text in a college course in social research. At the same time, it stands on its own, so if you simply have a layperson's interest in learning more about social research, you've come to the right place.

Let me begin with some personal comments on how this book came about. As I calculate such things, I've been a social scientist almost all my life. In fact, I conducted my first social survey several decades ago, at the age of six.

At the time, I was living in Stowe, Vermont. While Stowe would soon become one of the primary ski centers of the East Coast, it was then a small farming community of some 500 people. Downtown Stowe consisted of a Congregational church, two drug stores, three hardware stores, two filling stations, a hotel, and the town hall, which housed the post office, the library, the town clerk, and an auditorium where movies were shown on weekends. I didn't actually live in the urban center of Stowe but in the Lower Village about two miles south of the town. It would have been called a suburb, I suppose, if that term had been in use in Vermont in 1944.

Like many contemporary opinion polls, my first survey was launched in response to a pressing social issue. For as long as I could remember (which was not all that long, of course), I had idolized Gene Autry, the Singing Cowboy. Throughout my childhood, I rode the range with Gene Autry, singing along with the Sons of the Pioneers, saving cowgirls from mean hombres, and so forth. With the same six-year-old mentality that believed all people were white Protestants who thought America was best, I

1

imagined that everyone shared my view that Gene Autry was the greatest of all cowboys. This childlike faith was rudely challenged, however, when my cousin, Freddy, announced one day that Roy Rogers was better! I was simply astounded. I recognized that Roy Rogers was another good guy, and Dale Evans seemed nice enough—but better than the Singing Cowboy? Never!

The manner in which I chose to handle the situation antici-pated my later career as a social researcher. I decided to conduct a public opinion poll of the community to find out whether the great American people (those of Lower Village, Stowe, Vermont branch) preferred Gene Autry or Roy Rogers. I began with my Aunt Annie. In the interests of scientific integrity, I should say a word or two about my relationship with Aunt Annie. In retro-spect, it seems to me that the better part of her life was devoted to making me happy. She clearly took enormous pride in my accom-plishments, believed anything I told her, and would do anything she could to satisfy my every whim. This, then, is the woman I selected for my first interview on the topic: Who is the greatest cowboy in the world? After I explained my purpose in conducting the survey, mentioning how rotten Freddy was for saying that Roy Rogers was better than Gene Autry, Aunt Annie was ready to respond. "I vote for Gene Autry." So the survey was off to a great start, and I was ready to interview the rest of the Lower Village.

After two or three more votes for Gene Autry (I used up my other aunts in the early hours of the polling), I ran into the first vote for Roy Rogers. While that shocked me a bit, I was comforted by the knowledge that Gene was well out in front. Having exhausted my supply of indulgent aunts, however, I was now going door-to-door interviewing relative strangers. (In a town of 500, there are no total strangers.) Before long, the tide had turned. Roy Rogers was actually in the lead. Gene Autry, the Sing-ing Cowboy, idol of millions, was being disgraced, and I felt pow-erless to do anything about it. Then an idea burst into my mind: I would re-interview Aunt Annie! I interviewed her fifteen or twenty times in the next few days. God, she loved the delight in my eyes every time she said, "I vote for Gene Autry."

I am pleased to report that Gene Autry was found to be Amer-ica's favorite cowboy in the only known survey on the subject. I suspect this experience may have pushed me—unconsciously, to be sure—in the direction of a career in social research. Or maybe that early survey and my later career were both chosen for me by a higher power. (The Singing Cowboy is everywhere.)

My early brush with social research might suggest a neatly laid-out future, but that was hardly the case. My life has largely been a string of accidents, which began, as nearly as I can recall, on that stereotypical day in ninth grade when the teacher asked all the class: "What do you want to be when you grow up?" At that time, my mother had just remarried, following a divorce that left me fatherless for a dozen years or so. My new father was Herman Octave Babbie. I looked up to him as though I were trying to make up for all the years without a dad. I took his name, and I wanted to be just like him.

When the ninth-grade teacher, who was also our principal, asked our class about our career plans, I replied that I wanted to be an "auto-body man." I recall that the teacher didn't know what that was, until one of my classmates said it was a kind of mechanic. Indeed, Herman Babbie was an excellent auto-body mechanic, and I couldn't think of a nobler calling.

To his credit, my teacher didn't put me down or try to talk me out of my dream, but he did gently mention that since I did so well in school, I might consider going to college. I think I had some vague idea of what college was, but I had never considered going there. When I told my parents, they were very supportive, though they worried about what it might cost.

I had a new career plan now. Instead of being an auto body mechanic, I would become an engineer. That stayed with me as a low-grade aspiration throughout the remainder of junior high and high school. I would spend hours in my room drafting the designs for new inventions, like a hand-powered helicopter. (Great idea but it never got off the ground.)

We moved from Vermont to New Hampshire just before my sophomore year of high school, and I became more active in school activities, joined the debate team, and soon had my first "best friend," Charlie Crocco. Charlie was more sophisticated and more worldly than me. Among other things, he introduced me to the world of ideas and the world of jazz—both of which have continued to fascinate and entertain me throughout my life. When time finally came for us to apply to college, I was still essentially clueless, but Charlie was again my guide.

Charlie applied for a Navy ROTC scholarship to Harvard, so I did, too. Out of naiveté, not arrogance, I didn't apply anywhere else. I suppose if someone had asked me about applying to more than one college, I would have thought it was like proposing to several girls to see which ones would accept. Ultimately, both of us were accepted by Harvard. However, the Navy physicals we had to take showed that Charlie was color blind, which precluded him from being trained as a paid professional killer. Without the scholarship, he couldn't afford Harvard and went to Duke instead. (He returned to Cambridge a few years later for Harvard Law School.)

When I was accepted by Harvard, I really didn't know where it was, even though I lived only a couple of hours' drive away, in southern New Hampshire. Nonetheless, prior to the beginning of the fall 1956 semester my folks packed me into the family car, and off we went to Cambridge, Massachusetts, so I could pursue my new career path: becoming an engineer.

My four years at Harvard would present many problems. First, I was poor and many of my classmates came from great wealth. Second, I had been very successful in high school—I had been an almost straight-A student, president of the Student Council and the Debate Team, etc., but I soon discovered that everyone in my class had equally impressive or even more impressive credentials. Third, I quickly learned that the course of study I had mastered so easily and well wasn't nearly as rigorous as many of my classmates' secondary-school experiences. Many of them had read books, for example. In other words, I wasn't particularly well prepared for any college, let alone Harvard.

One problem I faced in the first week or so, however, was insurmountable: I had come to Cambridge to become an engineer and Harvard didn't offer engineering! Once my advisor had dropped this bomb, we discussed my interests and decided I should major in physics. Thus, my career ambition had evolved from auto body mechanics to engineering to nuclear physics. This seemed a reasonable shift to me, since I had done well in physics in high school.

Sure. My first semester, I enrolled in Physics, Calculus, German, and a couple of other courses. The normal load was four courses, but since one of mine was Naval Science, regarded as a gut course, I was allowed to take a slightly heavier load. That first semester at Harvard was many things for me. It was exciting and eye-opening in many ways, but it was also my first experience of almost total failure in academics.

The physics course, a general education introduction, not just for physics majors, was okay. I certainly didn't set any records in the course but I didn't feel totally stupid. I think I got a B or a C. Introductory German, the first half of a year-long course, was an utter disaster. At times, I wasn't sure the GIs in WWII Europe had as much trouble with the Germans as I was having. Itseemedtomethatpracticallywholesentenceswerejammedtogether insinglewords . . . gedanken. I'd never been especially good at foreign languages, but this was ridiculous. I got a C in the course; maybe a C–.

My downfall, however, was calculus. I had been not just good at math but enthusiastic about it for as long as I could remember. In second grade, our teacher gave us the essentials of Roman numerals and told us to write from 1 to 30. I quickly wrote to 100: XXXXXXXXXX. (We hadn't gotten to L and C.) Around fifth or sixth grade, an older friend taught me elementary algebra, and I thought it was the greatest thing ever invented. In preparation for a bus ride to Boston, I made up page after page of algebra problems that I would solve during the trip. In high school, I decided geometry eclipsed algebra as the greatest invention of the human mind. As I began confronting the challenges of my college experience, I was confident that mathematics would be my supportive friend.

Wrong. Calculus totally eluded me. As I think back on that devastating experience, I place most of the blame with a pesky new entity: delta (Δ). It was infinitesimally small, we were told. It had no height, width, depth, or weight. So it was zero, I surmised. No, I was corrected, delta was bigger than zero. So, how big was it? So was it a teeny little bit? No, not quite that big. Argh!

I recall that I got a C in the mid-term exam, which turned out to be the second highest grade in the class. Damning with faint praise? I didn't look forward to the final with much enthusiasm. In fact, I managed to convince myself that the three-hour morning final was actually in the afternoon. When I discovered my mistake, I rushed across campus to arrive at the exam with thirty minutes remaining.

"Who do I see about making up this exam?" I asked breathlessly. The exam proctor looked at me and asked, "Are you sick?"

"No, I thought the exam was this afternoon, instead of this morning."

"I'm afraid they won't let you take the exam later unless you are sick with a doctor's statement. There's still 30 minutes left. Why don't you sit down and do as much as you can."

So I took a seat, opened the exam, gasped, and began scribbling my best guess at the first step for solving each of the problems. Then I tried to scribble the second step. Soon the thirty minutes was up, and the proctor announced that the exam was over. All the other students turned in their exams, and the proctor said to me, "I'll give you another half hour." That was followed by another half hour—totaling an hour and a half of panicked calculus aversion.

Having failed calculus, added to my C– in German, my prospects were not the best. Things got worse when I took my advisor's advice and dropped German. As it turned out, that meant I lost all credit for the first semester of the year-long course. So I had completed four courses, getting an F in one of them.

As a Navy ROTC student, I took a Naval Science course in addition to my regular academic load. Partly because I received an A in that course, I barely dodged the bullet of being marched off the parade grounds in shackles or having the lock changed on my dorm room. It was pretty clear that I'd be shopping for a new college or a career that didn't require college. However, I had one more semester coming to me, so I shopped around for some courses to take.

I can't remember what prompted my signing up for Cultural Anthropology. Maybe it was a convenient hour. But I soon found myself in Professor Douglas Oliver's introduction to the sociocultural ways of humans and other primates. I was blown away by it. Mostly, I hadn't thought much about the ways in which cultures might differ. Much of my first year at Harvard was spent recovering from the unexamined belief that pretty much everyone was a white Protestant/Republican. I had arrived in Cambridge thinking everyone else was pretty much like me, only richer.

By the end of the semester, I had become a social scientist. At first I was committed to becoming an anthropologist, but I soon discovered Harvard had an amazing major with a terrible name: Social Relations. SocRel combined sociology with social psychology and social anthropology. Over the next three years, I took courses from the very top scholars in each of those three disciplines. As I improved my college skills, my grades improved and I became confident that I would actually graduate.

By my senior year, I had shifted my chief interest from anthropology to sociology. While the two fields had a great deal of overlap in concepts, theories, and methods, anthropology focused on preliterate societies whereas sociology focused more on modern ones. The main reason for my shift, however, was the influence of Talcott Parsons, arguably the leading sociologist on the planet at that time. Parsons was a prolific writer, and if you have never read any of his books, you might be advised not to do so.

Both his supporters and critics would probably agree that he was and is difficult to read and comprehend. And yet, strangely, I found him accessible and fascinating as a lecturer. Sometimes, I think he lectured pretty much the way he wrote, but he was just easier to understand in the flesh, at least for me.

Parsons had a way of presenting sociological concepts that worked powerfully for me. He might start by saying that a social status was a position people could occupy in the social grid—for example, occupations such as plumber, police officer, professor. Okay, I got it: statuses are occupations. Then, he would add that family positions would also be examples: father, mother, son, sister. Having initially created one image in my mind, he now forced me to stretch that image to include other categories of statuses. But wait, Protestant, Catholic, Jew, and Muslim were also statuses. More mental stretching. Other statuses, he might explain, could be liberals and conservatives, cancer patients, burglars, deadbeat dads, and on it went. Every time I felt I had a handle on a concept, he would complicate it and I would have to adapt. Ultimately, I felt I had a very robust grasp of important sociological concepts. I came back again and again, taking more courses from Talcott Parsons than from any other professor.

Senior year, I screwed up my courage to make an appointment to see the great man in his office, to discuss my plans to become a sociologist. I was a little nervous when I first sat down with him, and matters got worse when it became apparent that he thought I was interviewing him about the profession of sociologist, for a term paper or something. Finally, I stammered that I wanted to BE one.

"Oh, then, you should go to graduate school," he explained. I wrote that down in my notebook and asked, "Where should I go?"

"Somewhere else," he quickly replied.

He must have seen the shocked and crushed look on my face, as he added, "Everyone should go somewhere else. You shouldn't do all your studies in the same place with the same faculty."

Thus relieved, I asked, "Where should I go?" He thought a minute and said, "I don't know. Why don't you go to Berkeley?" I wrote that down and thanked him for his guidance.

Before I could continue my career path into sociology, there was the matter of my obligation to the NROTC program. In exchange for a generous scholarship (though I still needed a part-time job all four years), I owed the program three years of active duty service as an officer and a gentleman. Most of my service was in the Far East: Okinawa, Japan, even getting a glimpse of Vietnam from aboard ship as the war was heating up.

Three years later, I arrived at UC Berkeley with not much more of a plan than I had upon arriving at Harvard. At least I wasn't planning to major in engineering this time. I still remember arriving at South Hall on the Berkeley campus, then home of the Sociology Department. As I was checking in, one of the secretaries asked who I would like as my advisor. Big problem. Although it turned out that the department was made up of many of the biggest names in Sociology, I had no idea who was there. When I replied that I didn't know who I wanted, the secretaries asked what I was interested in. Since I'd been kind of interested in the sociology of religion at Harvard, I mentioned that, and I recall one secretary saying to the other, "Let's give him to Glock." That was good news to me, since I recalled having read an article he had written on the sociology of religion. So he was at Berkeley. Neat.

Through the mere chance of saying I was interested in the sociology of religion, I met Charles Young Glock, who would become my advisor, mentor, employer, co-author, and friend. My first semester at Berkeley, I served as Charlie's underpaid ($200 for the semester) assistant ("reader") in his course, the Sociology of Religion. In 1965 I published my first journal article in a special edition of the *Review of Religious Research* (which Charlie edited). And in 1967 I co-authored (with Charlie and Benjamin Ringer) my first book: a study of Episcopalians entitled *To Comfort and to Challenge*.

That was the extent of our collaboration in the sociology of religion and pretty much the extent of my research in that field. However, Charlie Glock was mainly known for something else: survey research. Consistent with the theme of this essay, Charlie had gotten into survey research by chance. He was at Columbia University, either completing or having just completed an MBA, when he happened to meet Paul Lazarsfeld, one of the most important pioneers in survey research. Lazarsfeld had moved his research center from Princeton to Columbia and renamed it the Bureau of Applied Social Research. He told Charlie that the Bureau needed someone with business training to run it, and he offered the job to Charlie. Thus, Charlie Glock became the new director of BASR and earned a PhD in Sociology in the process.

During the 1950s, a national review of colleges and universities confirmed the exalted status of the University of California at Berkeley. In field after field, it ranked Number One or in the immediate vicinity, yet sociology was one field where it was sorely lacking. Thus, UCB went to the University of Chicago and hired a well-respected scholar, Herbert Blumer, to whom they essentially gave a blank checkbook and told him to buy a first-class sociology faculty.

It is worth noting that Herb Blumer was not a well-rounded or even mainstream sociologist. He was a flag bearer of the "Chicago School" established by George Herbert Mead, Charles Horton Cooley, and others during the 1920s through the 1940s. Their sociological orientation focused on the study of social interaction and community studies. When Blumer received his charge from Berkeley, however, the field of sociology was moving in quite different directions nationally—for example, the "Grand Theories" of Talcott Parsons and others, and quantitative studies such as mass opinion surveys. When I later studied under Blumer at Berkeley, I found he could debunk and disclaim such approaches with passion.

As I understand it, however, the Blumer hiring hall was anything but narrow-minded. While he fundamentally disagreed with Talcott Parsons, he recognized Parsons' prominence in the field and felt Berkeley needed the best possible Parsonian they could find. He hired Neil Smelser, a student of Parsons' and subsequently one of the most prominent sociologists in his own right. Blumer thought quantitative studies such as survey research were basically wrong-headed, but he also recognized sociology was moving in that direction, so he reached out for the best he could find. He stole Charlie Glock from Columbia's Bureau of Applied Social Research and gave Glock the assignment of creating a Survey Research Center.

So, having been assigned Charlie Glock as my advisor, because of our mutual interest in the sociology of religion, I was sent to meet him at the Survey Research Center. At the time, I had no idea what survey research was.

Another of Glock's responsibilities was to teach the two introductory courses in research methods for graduate students. Ironically, in 1963 and 1964 when I took these courses, he was replaced by visiting faculty members. So while he would become my mentor, co-author, and my closest friend among the faculty, I never studied research methods from Glock. Years later, when my textbook on survey research was virtually the only text being used in American survey research classes, my son, Aaron, would take that course from virtually the only faculty member not using my book. In fact, he gave no indication of recognizing Aaron's last name.

I've already mentioned that I worked as a reader in Glock's undergraduate course in the sociology of religion during my first semester of graduate school at Berkeley. I had arrived with some money in the bank, my savings from three years of service in the USMC. By the end of the first semester, all my money was gone and I asked Glock for a more substantial job. As a result, I became a research assistant, earning $200 a month, which was enough for a Berkeley graduate student at that time if you drank generic wine.

My new job gave me my first direct contact with survey research, which I learned as one of Charlie Glock's apprentices over the next five years or so. Since Charlie had learned survey research in a similar fashion from social research pioneer Paul Lazarsfeld, I came to think of Lazarsfeld as my intellectual grandfather, which I got to tell him the one time I actually met him.

Glock put me to work on a variety of projects he was involved with at the time. The first of these—a study of attitudes toward racial integration in Berkeley—resulted in my first sociological paper, co-authored with Charlie and Bob Rankin, a visiting scholar. Other projects provided experience that would figure importantly in my later writing about research methods. One major project, a national survey of medical school faculty members, would serve as my doctoral dissertation, later published by the University of California Press as *Science, Morality, and Medicine.*

My work at SRC became a major focus of my graduate studies, and I actually ended up serving as Assistant Director my final year. Survey research was also the key to my first job after graduation. In 1967 or 1968, Professor Doug Yamamura, chairman of the Sociology Department at the University of Hawaii, visited Charlie Glock to seek his advice. Doug explained that UH wanted to create a Survey Research Center, and they hoped Charlie could advise them on how to go about it. As I recall, Charlie's advice was, "Hire someone like Earl, who knows about survey research and is just getting started, and have him do it." So, in 1968, I found myself on the faculty of the University of Hawaii, running a fledgling program in survey research (mostly consulting) and teaching a graduate seminar in the subject.

Teaching was a brand new experience for me. As a graduate student, I'd been a research assistant rather than a teaching assistant—hence I had never taught a course. In recent years, many graduate departments have created courses or programs to teach graduate students how to teach, but in my era we were expected to figure it out.

I recall my first course at UH. It was scheduled in a room that would hold about 40 students, with a desk and chair on a platform for the instructor. I had six students. It was two weeks before I stopped sitting behind the desk on the platform at the front of the room. Finally, I suggested that we meet in my office, where I had books and other resources we could use. One of the major challenges I faced was the selection of a textbook for the course. There weren't any very good ones, and I ended up using a British textbook, despite the Brits' inability to spell English correctly.

One day, I found myself sketching out a table of contents for what I was calling "A Survey Research Cookbook and Other Fables." This reflected the existence of some textbooks that would provide detailed descriptions of a particular survey, which would be of little use if you wished to do a survey in a different situation. The next day, I received a letter from Wadsworth Publishing Company saying that they wanted to publish a survey research textbook and their consulting editor, Rod Stark, my best friend in graduate school, had recommended me. I sent my table of contents by return mail (no e-mail then, but we had airplanes) and I soon had a contract to write my first textbook.

Writing what was renamed *Survey Research Methods* was a brand new experience for me. It was a little like teaching a course, except I was writing everything down instead of saying it. And it turned out that grammar and stuff like that were important. (Who knew?) In part, writing the book meant putting on paper things that I already knew. However, the act of writing had an understandable though unpredicted effect. I got to know those things more clearly and maybe more profoundly than before. This was followed months later by a stranger effect. Inevitably, although some of the advice I gave to beginning survey researchers represented my best judgment, I realized others might disagree. When I saw my advice in print, however, it seemed *True*.

This phenomenon has gotten stranger still over the years, especially as I've written less specialized textbooks—social research in general and introductory sociology, for example. Most of the content of *Survey Research Methods* derived from my personal experience. But writing the more general books required me to learn new research techniques, new concepts, and new bodies of knowledge, which, since I've always loved learning, has been a side benefit of writing textbooks. However, I have frequently mastered some topic, written about it for a textbook, and then, through disuse, pretty much forgotten it. When a need arises to know about that topic later on, I return to what I had written in a textbook, unconsciously regarding that as the *Truth*, the way you'd trust something you looked up in an encyclopedia. This could be the introduction to a chapter on the sociology of knowledge, but that's not the purpose of this essay.

My purpose in this lengthy introduction is to impress upon you the unplanned and even accidental process that led an aspiring auto-body mechanic to grapple with issues of social science research. As I write these words, I am far nearer the end of my career than I am to its beginning, and yet I feel I am still scratching the surface of some profound questions about life and how we study it. The essays that follow lay out some of the puzzles that have interested me, and I hope you will find them worth attempting to solve.

PART 1

AN INTRODUCTION TO INQUIRY

1

Closed Answers and Open Questions

If I were to say that the job of the scientist is to find answers to questions, probably not many people would disagree. After all, don't the great discoveries of science take the form of answers to such questions as, "What makes objects fall to earth? Why is the sky blue? What causes rain? What causes cancer? How can we unlock the power of the atom?"

In conventional instruction in scientific methods, students are taught that a scientist begins with a question, specifies the exact meanings of the elements contained in the question, and designs experiments that reveal the relationships among those elements. By this process, a taxing question gets displaced by a definitive answer; ignorance gives way to knowledge and we can all go to the beach.

I can't say how well this description fits the natural sciences, but it rules out much of the power of social science. This is not to say that social scientists never operate in the fashion described above or that nothing of value is ever discovered that way. Researchers who ask whether discrimination against women in the American labor force still exists find, among other things, that women earn only about three-fourths of what men earn. Those who ask why the gender gap in pay exists find that it cannot be accounted for on the basis of training, experience, or similar reasonable explanations. This is useful to know.

Still, the image of scientists finding answers to carefully framed questions misrepresents much of the scientific enterprise, at least in social science. An instructive way to begin is by recognizing that everything we know today is likely to be overturned at some point in the future. It is ironic that we understand the process involved in developing human knowledge throughout human history (and presumably throughout human prehistory) and yet assume that what we know today is pretty much immune to that process.

Skipping over eons of early explanations for the heavenly bodies, we know that the Ptolemaic system of astronomy placed the earth at the center of the universe. In one important specific, it held that the sun revolved around the earth. As the Ptolemaic system of circular epicycles became more refined, scholars were able to predict the movement of stars and planets quite accurately.

Today, of course, we look back on the Ptolemaic system as erroneous. Thanks to Copernicus and Kepler, we know that the earth and the other planets in our solar system revolve around the sun and that they travel in elliptical rather than circular paths. We look upon the pre-Copernicans as being in error, though we may be fairly civil and generous in the matter. I sometimes feel a little paternalistic in forgiving our ancestors for making such mistakes, as though they were children who just didn't know any better. The way we now see things seems manifestly accurate, right, and true. After all, the earth does revolve around the sun. There may still be things we don't know, but we've at least got that one right, haven't we?

Let's stay with the relative movement of the earth and the sun for a moment longer. Since the time of Einstein, we know that their movements are just that: relative. As seen from the sun, the earth would seem to move. As seen from somewhere else in the universe, both the sun and the earth seem to move.

When we limit our attention to the solar system, as though the whole system were fixed in space, the notion that the sun is stationary with the planets moving around it in elliptical paths is a useful one. It allows us to explain why a particular planet arrives at a particular spot relative to the sun at a particular time and to predict where it will go next. Moreover, the whole thing fits comfortably within our current systems of mathematics, geometry, logic, and so forth. All this argues for keeping the view we currently have regarding the relative movements of the earth and the sun, but it does not guarantee that later generations won't look back on us as misguided children.

We have no way of knowing whether what we now know will stand the test of time. The odds are that it won't. In his *The Half-Life of Facts* (2012), Samuel Arbesman has carefully examined how long the established "facts" of various scientific disciplines stand the test of time before being overturned by new discoveries. Arbesman cites a 2002 study that calculated the half-life of medical knowledge about hepatitis and cirrhosis of the liver to be 45 years. That is, half of what scientists "knew" in this field was outdated or disproven in 45 years. In a broader analysis, Ron Tang (2002:361) researched scientific journals to determine the half-life of knowledge in other fields. He reported the following:

- Religion: 8.76 years
- History: 7.13 years
- Psychology: 7.15 years
- Economics: 9.38 years
- Math: 9.17 years
- Physics: 13.07 years

The tenuousness of answers is probably far greater in social science than in the natural sciences. This reflects our subject matter rather than the strength or weakness of our methods. Society is a *recursive* phenomenon: we engage in the same business over and over, day in and day out. However, the way we do things today is importantly affected by our experiences from yesterday, and our methods tomorrow will be influenced by our experiences both yesterday and today. Whenever we reach an answer to some question about human social life, our possession of that answer is likely to have an impact on the nature of social life itself, possibly to the extent of invalidating the answer. Let's consider a few examples.

Having sexual intercourse causes women to get pregnant. Pregnancy has never been an automatic consequence of sex, but if a woman has sex often enough and does not take countermeasures, she is likely to get pregnant. At some point in our distant history, people didn't know that. They only knew that women sometimes got pregnant. It seems probable, therefore, that people used to ask the question, "Why do women get pregnant?"

Eventually, we learned the answer to the question, and our knowledge grew until we found ways of lessening the likelihood of pregnancy: the rhythm method, condoms, birth control pills, sterilization, and so forth. With the advent of artificial insemination, moreover, it became possible for women to get pregnant without having sex. In the long run, then, answering the question, "Why do women get pregnant?" actually weakened the validity of that particular answer.

The Protestant ethic, of which the sociologist Max Weber wrote, provides another example of the recursive quality of answers in human society. The theologian John Calvin asserted in the 1500s that whether a person would go to heaven after death was preordained by God. In Calvin's view, nothing could change that.

People who subscribed to Calvin's view were naturally more than a little curious to know whether or not they were going to heaven, even though they couldn't do anything about it. They found the answer in Calvinistic beliefs about the natural conduct of those chosen by God. In general, it was expected that the chosen would work hard during their stay on earth, apply themselves, use their money wisely, and so forth. By contrast, those who lived immoral, wanton lives and spent their money on worldly pleasures were undoubtedly headed toward an unhappy reward. Since all of Calvin's followers wanted to be sure they were going to heaven, it was especially important that they work hard and prosper. As a consequence, they saved their money, invested it, reinvested the profits, and created capitalism.

Thus, once people had the answer to the question, "How will we know if we are going to heaven?" they reacted in ways that destroyed the objective validity of the answer. If hard work and material success had once been independent, objective measures of God's plans for the soul, it ceased to be so when multitudes began actively pursuing it as a proof of salvation.

Marxism offers another illustration of the recursive aspect of social life and knowledge about it. Marx's studies of history pointed to particular relationships among social classes, and he assembled a mass of evidence to support his views. Once his views of how social classes related to one another were widely disseminated, however, radical shifts occurred in those relationships. Even in places where no particular effort to change class relationships was made, they changed by virtue of public knowledge of the issue. Today, many scholars speak of Marx's theory of the class struggle as being outdated.

The "bandwagon effect" in the arena of public opinion is another example. Social researchers conduct surveys to answer the question, "What percentage of voters will vote for Candidate X?" If a large majority of those polled say they will vote for Candidate X, the report of that result encourages others to vote the same way. If only a small minority say they will vote for Candidate X, the poll results shift additional voters away from that candidate.

Two points emerge from all this:

- Our knowledge is tenuous. Anything we "know" today may be overturned by new discoveries tomorrow.

• Anything we learn about human social life can have an impact on what we are studying, even to the extent of invalidating what we learned in the first place.

Our normal way of responding to questions is to answer them, thus closing the lines of inquiry they represent. Or if we think questions can't be answered, logic suggests that we avoid them altogether. For social researchers, a more powerful method is appropriate: to hold them as *open questions* and to continue asking them, even when no definitive answers seem possible. The purpose of this is to keep lines of inquiry open.

Perhaps the greatest contribution can be made by keeping questions open when everyone else seems to feel they have been answered. After all, it wasn't so very long ago that just about everyone "knew" men were superior to women. And everyone (well, all the white people) "knew" whites were superior to blacks; in fact, blacks weren't even considered fully human. Fortunately, a few people were at least willing to consider such matters as open questions; and that's a special opportunity for social researchers.

Social science deals with a set of topics that most people already have fixed opinions about. I've already mentioned the matters of racial and sexual equality. Much of my own early research was in the sociology of religion. A typical research question was, "Why are some people more religious than others?" For some people deeply involved in religion, the answer is already known—though different people know different answers. For some, varying degrees of religiosity are simply a reflection of people's being fundamentally good or evil. For others, the answer lies in whether or not people have been called to religion by God. Research findings that women are more religious than men, that old people are more religious than young people, and so forth, make no sense to such people.

Another typical research question in the sociology of religion involves the function of organized religion in society. Again, for many people, the answer to that question is obvious. For example, they may believe that churches have the job of showing people the "right" way to be. Or they may feel that churches are a vehicle for determining rewards and punishments in an afterlife. Again, social scientific notions such as "social solidarity" or "institutional integration" may seem irrelevant to them.

Similar comments could be made regarding almost anything social scientists study. You may think that education is a good thing; social scientists ask whether it is and in what ways. You may think that deviance (crime, for example) is bad, but social scientists also examine the positive functions of deviance: innovation and social change, for example. The power of social research, then, lies more in the realm of questions than in the realm of answers. Much has been said elsewhere about the importance of framing good questions in research, and while that's accurate, I mean something more profound.

A number of big questions about human social life will probably never be answered. The so-called nature-versus-nurture debate is a good example: are human social characteristics more a product of genetics or of social learning, more a matter of inheritance or of social conditioning? A vast body of research on the sources of intelligence has not answered the question in favor of one side or the other. In all likelihood, no future research will answer the basic question.

The primary purpose of this book of essays is to open up similar questions in the area of social research. These include, among others:

- *Chapter 2*: Can we ever be truly objective? Does truth even exist? Is reality just a matter of agreement?

- *Chapter 4*: Do human beings possess free will? Are we able to shape our own destinies, or are we determined by forces and factors beyond our control?

- *Chapter 5*: Does prejudice really exist? How do we know? Where is it located?

- *Chapter 8*: Do social researchers observe and study people's attitudes or actually create them?

- *Chapter 15*: Is social science really scientific? Is it perhaps the first science?

These are but a few of the questions we'll be exploring. Be forewarned that we won't be answering all of them, but you won't be bored. Moreover, I think you'll find yourself increasingly willing and able to deal with open questions as we proceed. If so, you will have become that much more capable of experiencing the thrill of social research.

2

Truth, Objectivity, and Agreement

Science is often portrayed as a search for the truth about reality. That sounds good, but what is truth? What is reality? Look those words up in a good dictionary, such as the *Oxford English Dictionary*, and you'll find definitions like "the quality of being true" and "the quality of being real." Beyond these basic tautologies are some additional definitions (from the *OED*):

Truth:
- Conformity with fact; agreement with reality
- Agreement with a standard or rule; accuracy, correctness
- Genuineness, reality, actual existence
- That which is in accordance with fact
- That which is true, real, or actual; reality

Reality:
- The quality of . . . having an actual existence
- Correspondence to fact; truth
- Real existence

Definitions of the words *true* and *real* are similar:

True:
- Consistent with fact; agreeing with reality; representing the thing as it is
- Agreeing with a standard, pattern, or rule; exact, accurate, precise, correct, right
- Consistent with, exactly agreeing with

- Conformable to reality; natural
- In accordance with reality

Real:

- Having an objective existence; actually existing as a thing
- Actually present or existing as a state or quality of things; having a foundation in fact; actually occurring or happening
- Consisting of actual things

These definitions point to the inherent circularity of language, which is inevitable as long as we use words to define words. In this case, things are true if they're real and real if they're true. The relationship between truth and reality can also be seen in the preponderance of words dealing with agreement: conformity, accordance, correspondence, consistent with, representing.

Here's a useful way of seeing the relationship between truth and reality: it is possible to make statements about reality; those that agree with (conform to, are consistent with, represent) reality are true. None of this tells us what truth or reality is, however. It only tells us about their relationship to one another. Other words in the definitions we've seen may clarify the meanings of truth and reality—words such as actual, existence, and fact.

Actuality:

- The state of being actual or real; reality, existing objective fact

Actual:

- Existing in act or fact; really acted or acting; carried out; real

Factual:

- Pertaining to or concerned with facts; of the nature of fact, actual, real

Fact:

- Something that has really occurred or is actually the case
- Truth attested by direct observation or authentic testimony; reality

Existence:

- Actuality; reality
- Being; the fact or state of existing

Exist:

• To have place in the domain of reality, have objective being

By now, the incestuous circularity of language is getting a little annoying. Consider this abbreviated search for truth:

Truth is "that which is real; reality."

Reality is "having an actual existence."

Existence is "actuality; reality."

Actuality is "existing objective fact."

Fact is "truth attested by direct observation."

In addition to the circularity of these relatively few words defining each other, let's take a cue from the definitions of exist and existence and add the term *being*.

Being:

• Existence

• That which exists or is conceived as existing

Be:

• To have or take place in the world of fact; to exist, occur, happen

• To have place in the objective universe or realm of fact, to exist

• To come into existence

• To be the case or the fact

For the most part, these new words simply add to the circularity of definitions that is becoming very familiar in this exercise. Figure 2.1 on the following page illustrates this.

From time to time throughout these definitions, and now in the definition of *be*, the quality of objectivity has appeared as part of the background of a definition. In these cases, *real* does not just have existence, it has "objective existence"; *actuality* is not just a matter of fact but of "objective fact." Now, to be is to have a place in the "objective universe." Implicit in these uses is the contrast between objectivity and subjectivity.

Subjectivity:

• The quality or condition of viewing things exclusively through the medium of one's own mind or individuality

• The character of existing in the mind only

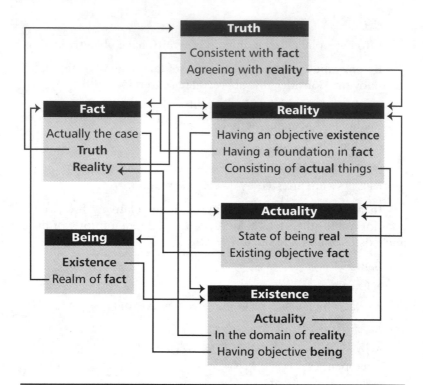

Figure 2.1   The Circular Meaning of Words

Subjective:

• Relating to the thinking subject, proceeding from or taking place within the subject; having its source in the mind

In stark contrast, objective is defined this way:

Objective:

• That which is external to the mind

The truth about truth eventually comes down to the recognition that we know most of the world through our minds. Moreover, we recognize that our individual minds are not altogether reliable. We have colloquial phrases such as "a figment of your imagination," and we realize that people often "see what they want to see." Simply put, the subjective realm refers to the possibly inaccurate perceptions and thoughts we have through the medium of our minds, yours and mine, whereas the objective realm refers to that which lies outside and is independent of our minds. We often term that objective realm *reality*, and term *true* a statement that accurately describes reality.

A couple of snags lie hidden in this construction of objectivity. First, neither you nor I, perceiving reality through our subjective minds, can know whether or not we perceive it accurately. The following scene should make the matter painfully clear.

Imagine that you are sitting in a room that has a small window with a view into another room. A light located in the other room can be turned on or off. Reality in this illustration is simply whether the light is on or off in the other room. Truth is a function of your ability to say accurately whether the light is on or off.

At first impression, nothing could be simpler. I turn the light on in the other room, and you say, "The light is on." I turn it off, and you say, "The light is off." This would be a model of objectivity.

The defect in this model is that your mind and its subjectivity have not been taken into account. But imagine that the small window before you has two shutters. The first shutter has a picture of the other room with the light on, and the second has a picture of the room with the light off. Sometimes the first shutter will close your view of the other room, sometimes the second shutter will, and sometimes there won't be any shutter—but you'll never know.

Now when I ask you whether the light is on in the other room, you will answer based on what you see, but what you see may be the open window or it may be one of the shutters. If you see one of the shutters, the scene you see may correspond with the real condition of the room or it may not.

Relating this illustration to real life, however, you would not be conscious of the possibility that you were looking at a shutter; instead, you would think that what you perceived was reality. You would feel sure that you knew the truth about whether the light was on or off because you saw it with your own eyes. And even if you became aware of the existence of the shutters, you couldn't be sure of reality because you still wouldn't know if what you were seeing was the other room or one of the shutters. The point of this illustration is that you have no way out. In the normal course of life, you cannot be sure that what you see is really there. But there's a bigger problem than this. Given the subjectivity of your mind, you can't be sure there is anything out there at all. In the two-room illustration, maybe there is no window and no other room—only two shutters. Maybe it's all in your mind. How could you ever know?

The answer to both of these dilemmas is the same. If you can't be sure that what your mind tells you is true, you can at least gain some confidence in that regard if you find that my mind has told me the same thing. You say the light is on, and I say the light is on: case closed. Now you may feel doubly sure you know the light is on, not to mention that there's a window, a room, and a light.

Ultimately, our only proof of objectivity is intersubjectivity, and some dictionaries even define objectivity that way. When different subjects—with their individual, error-prone subjectivities—report the same thing, we conclude that what they report is objective, existing, actual, factual, real, and true.

Thus, the basis of truth is agreement. Basically, things are true if we agree they are. When Copernicus first said that the earth revolved around the sun, few people agreed; today, most people agree. We say that this view is not only true today but was true when Copernicus first expressed it, and it was even true before Copernicus. But we say all that today when virtually everyone agrees with the view. Moreover, if all the world's astronomers were to announce a new discovery showing the sun revolved around the earth, we'd soon be saying that Copernicus was wrong and that the sun had always revolved around the earth, even before Copernicus.

When you think about the past history of agreements that were eventually overturned, you won't find much basis for confidence in what you and I now agree to be so. As discussed in Chapter 1, most of what we "know" today will be thrown out as inaccurate tomorrow.

Where does science figure in all this? What about social science? Doesn't it offer an exception to this? Isn't it a dependable channel to the truth?

Ultimately, science—social or otherwise—also operates on the basis of agreement: in this case, agreement among fellow scientists. But there are some differences. Scientists recognize that knowledge is continually changing. They realize that what they know today may be replaced tomorrow. In fact, the goal of science is to keep changing the truth. Scientists are aware of the power of subjective biases and are explicitly committed to avoiding them in their research. Social researchers have an advantage in this respect, since bias itself is subject matter for social science. On the other hand, social researchers have a disadvantage in that their subject matter—religion and politics, for example—is more likely to provoke personal biases than is the subject matter of the natural sciences.

For scientists, observation is a conscious and deliberate activity, whereas it is generally casual and semiconscious for most people in normal life. Thus, you might mistakenly recall that your best friend wore a blue dress yesterday, when it was really green. If you had been recording dress colors as part of a research project, however, you wouldn't have made that mistake.

Moreover, scientists have developed procedures and equipment to aid them in making observations. This also avoids some of the mistakes we make in casual observations. For example, scientists are explicit about the basis for their agreements. Rules of proof are contained within the system of logic prevailing at the time.

More important, perhaps, in the context of this essay, scientists are explicit about the intersubjective nature of truth. Peer review is an established principle: scientists review each other's work to guard against errors of method or reasoning. Scientific journals perform what is called a gatekeeper function in this regard. Articles submitted for publication are typically circulated among independent reviewers—other scientists knowledgeable in the area covered by the article. Unless the reviewers agree that the article represents a sound and worthwhile contribution to the field, it will not be published.

Scientists are by no means above error, however. Being human, they are susceptible to all the human foibles that afflict non-scientists. Though the scientific enterprise commits them to keeping an open mind with regard to truth, individual scientists can grow attached to particular views. We'll examine this issue in some detail in Chapter 13.

To understand the nature of science, it is essential to recognize that scientific knowledge at any given time is what scientists agree it is. Because scientific proof is fundamentally based on agreement among scientists, scientific knowledge keeps changing over time. It is probably unavoidable that we see this evolution of scientific knowledge over time as a process through which we get closer and closer to the truth. This view cannot be verified, however. All we can know for sure is that what we know keeps changing. We can't even bank on views that haven't changed for a long time. Bear in mind, for example, that the idea that the earth was stationary and the sun moved was accepted much longer than our current view has been. Years ago, when I was living in a house on the slopes of a volcano in Hawaii, I took comfort in knowing that the volcano hadn't erupted for 25,000 years and hence probably wouldn't ever erupt again. Then I learned that its previous period of dormancy had been longer than that.

In the case of scientific knowledge, changes are generally occurring faster, not slower, than in the past. And finally, as we saw in Chapter 1, what we learn about social life is often changed just by having the knowledge we've gained. On the whole, then, we'd do better simply to settle for the thrill of discovery than to worry about whether what we've discovered is the ultimate truth or simply a new and currently useful way of viewing things.

Ultimately, what we hold to be true is a matter of agreement. In 1977 I published an introductory sociology textbook, *Society by Agreement*. As far as textbook publishing is concerned, it was a success. However, it did not transform the teaching of sociology, as I had intended.

As I was getting ready to revise the book for the second edition, I received a call from Wadsworth's national sales meeting, presenting a request from the field representatives (the salespeople who visit campuses, meet with faculty, and promote their textbooks). Would I please change the title to something like, well, *Sociology*, or maybe *Introducing Sociology*. The current title sounded as though it was based on a conscious consensus among the members of a society, they said. At the least, it sounded like a book with a special point of view rather than offering a comprehensive view of sociology and society.

At first I was annoyed, since I really liked *Society by Agreement*. Then I did a little personal reflection as a professor. From time to time, I taught a course in social problems, and I had not written a textbook for that course. As a result, I would typically receive 15–20 textbooks from publishers seeking an adoption for my course. Being honest with myself, I had to admit that my first step usually involved culling out all the books that looked different from the standard. Some focused on a subset of social problems. Others espoused a particular theoretical paradigm. I tended to set these books aside right away, since I wanted to offer a comprehensive coverage of the field. I couldn't honestly blame either the field reps or the instructors if *SBA* was getting passed over early in the selection process. So I changed the title to *Sociology*. In three editions, the book sold about 100,000 copies, which is very good for a textbook, but each edition became more and more like all other textbooks with that title. When I stared into the yawning maw (whatever that is) of the fourth edition, I called it a day and let the book die. Mostly, I have regretted my failure to communicate the agreement theme effectively. So here's one final attempt to do so.

When I speak of "agreement," I mean it in more of a mathematical sense than in the sense of "coming to an agreement" or "reaching an agreement." In mathematics, we say that the two sides of an equation agree in the sense that they are the same or equal. So, a society by agreement is one in which our views about things are the same. And 99% of the time, those agreements are not the result of conscious debates, conversations, or negotiations.

If you and I agree that people need to wear clothes in public, that's because we were taught, early on, that people need to wear clothes in public. This is a process sociologists call socialization, which I defined as teaching/learning the agreements. This is the process by which a given society stays more or less the same over time.

While we agree on many, many things, we also disagree on some things. The greater the agreement, the more stable a society is; with less agreement, it is more unstable. And, of course, societies change over time. We call it social change: the changing of agreements prevailing in a society. Some of the fundamental aspects of social structure can be reframed in terms of agreements.

- Norms are agreements about what is expected of us.

- Values are agreements about what's better than something else.

- Beliefs are agreements about what's real.

Most fundamental sociological concepts can be expressed in the language of agreements. Social control is the enforcement of the agreements, and deviance is a matter of breaking the agreements. Culture is the collection of agreements generally shared among a society or sub-set of society.

One of the problems I think people have with using the metaphor of agreement for organizing the study of society was mentioned at the outset: the assumption that agreements are the result of voluntary consent. You say, "Let's go the movies Monday night," and I agree. Actually, most of the agreements that make up a society were here long before you and I arrived on the scene. Nobody asked me what language I would prefer to use. The agreement on English predated my birth, and I was initiated into it at an early age. In my use of the term, agreement, I entered into the pre-existing agreement on English as the predominant language where I was growing up, even though I never thought I had a choice. Presumably, I could have chosen to speak French or make up my own language, but I agreed to go along with the crowd.

To complicate matters, however, there is some value in regarding social agreements as a matter of consent. Here's an example I use with students. I point out that our society has an agreement that we must wear clothes in public. That's an agreement made well before any of my students were born. And yet, I suggest, that agreement can also be seen as the result of a public opinion poll—one they participated in! I point out that each of them voted in favor of clothes in public when they left home for school this morning. And look how it turned out: 100% in favor of clothes—again.

That's how societies survive: by members' willingness to vote repeatedly to keep things the same, day after day, generation after generation. And it has always been my feeling that there was a special power in this view. If you regard the established elements of society as agreements rather than "the way things are," the possibility of breaking and/or changing those agreements is enhanced.

For generations, first slavery and then blacks sitting in the back of the bus were regarded as the way things were, had always been, and would always be; there was no space for social change. You may have trouble understanding the certainty with which people believed such things to be inevitable. However, I'm sure there are things you believe with that degree of certainty. Perhaps you have firm religious beliefs or unshakable beliefs about social issues such as abortion or homosexuality.

Or, consider something really outrageous. We humans agree that we are unable to swim underwater, breathing in water and extracting the oxygen as fish do. Everybody believes that. You could ask around. So how do you feel about the possibility of violating that limitation? Not likely.

That's how people have felt about such things as slavery and segregation. And if you regard them as immutable, you are not likely to do anything to change matters. Once you recognize them as agreements, you are empowered to create different agreements.

I conclude this chapter by pursuing a little further the matter of how agreements are created. *Autopoiesis* is typically defined as "self-creating." I've always found some linguistic examples useful in seeing what this means. Suppose some fellow tells you he is sorry for something he said or did. How do you interpret that communication? Depending on your experiences with and understanding of the speaker, you might say to yourself, "Maybe he is, maybe he isn't." Certainly as a logical possibility, someone can say he is sorry without actually being sorry.

But suppose the same person said, "I apologize." This is a powerfully different communication. You can't logically say, "No, he didn't really apologize." Maybe he's not sorry, but he undeniably apologized. Saying "I apologize" brings the act of apologizing into existence. The statement creates its own truth. It creates itself.

Similarly, when a member of the clergy, a judge, or a justice of the peace says, "I pronounce you husband and wife," that pronouncement is automatically true (assuming they were certified to marry people). The same is true when the jury declares, "We find the defendant guilty." Notice that a member of the jury might say, "We found the defendant guilty" and be lying if the jury didn't actually reach a guilty verdict. However, when that jury member announces the verdict in court, it becomes true by saying it.

This chapter is not about a linguistic oddity, however. It goes deeper than that. Let me begin by acknowledging the Chilean biologist, Humberto Maturana, who introduced the term autopoesis as a defining characteristic of "life." When I had the opportunity of hearing Maturana lecture on the subject in the 1980s, I confess that I wasn't really able to follow his main arguments about life, but it was immediately clear to me that society was clearly autopoietic, and I felt that conceptualization might be useful in our understanding how society functions.

Let's return to an example mentioned earlier in this chapter, one I have used with sociology students over the years. I begin by pointing out that in our society we have an agreement (a norm) that people must wear clothes when they go out in public. No matter how hot it may be, we operate under a no-nudity rule. I've always thought I was doing my students a service by pointing out a rule that they need to obey or suffer the consequences, but most of them seem to have known that already.

"When was that rule enacted?" I ask. "And who did it?"

This sometimes causes confusion in the class. Well, it always does, actually. Nobody knows. There are probably lots of local ordinances about "indecent exposure," but none of my students (nor I) have actually read any of those ordinances. I have yet to have a student who would admit to having tested the rule and paid the price.

After some discussion of when anti-nudity rules were enacted, I suggested they were actually created the morning of our discussion. "There was a plebiscite this morning. We all voted, and this is how it turned out: 100% for clothes again. So, actually, YOU are the ones who created the rule and you did it this morning. All of you did it; nobody is exempted. Me, too, by the way."

I ask students to imagine what it would have been like if the vote had gone differently. Suppose it was a hot, muggy day, and we all voted against wearing clothes. Everyone would have voted by showing up naked, and that would have been the agreement for today. If everybody did it, of course, it's unlikely that anyone would have been punished, because nobody would be breaking the new rule. But since it's unlikely that everyone would have suddenly decided to go naked on the same day, let's imagine 10 people voted that way. They would have been punished, no doubt, and that would mean the rest of us, by voting for clothes and by punishing the dissenters, were re-creating the rule of wearing clothes.

But how about if 10 percent voted in the minority? Though it may look like a small percentage, that's a lot of naked people. The police don't constitute 10 percent of the population, so they would be outnumbered by naked people. In New York City, for example, the police force is equal to about half a percent of the eight million population. That would amount to about 20 naked people per police officer. Not a pretty sight. Or maybe it is, depending on your point of view. In any event, the police would be overwhelmed by 10 percent of the population breaking a law all at once.

On the other hand, the naked people would be outnumbered 9 to 1 by people wearing clothes: a powerful social-control force. Those clothed civilians wouldn't even have to make citizen arrests; pointing and giggling would probably work in many cases. Righteous indignation might get some of the nudists back into the fold. Or the threat of violence; naked = vulnerable. It could have turned out differently, however. Depending on how hot and humid it was, the people who initially voted for clothes might reconsider. And the more who shed their clothes, the more pressure and/or permission the rest would feel. Could happen.

In either event, it should be clear that the rules by which we live are enacted every day by those of us who feel bound by those rules. To be sure, such rules sometimes get codified and enacted into law, so it would be possible to say who did it and when. But the central point here is that society is an entity which creates itself; it is an autopoietic phenomenon.

While this view violates our implicit, unexamined ideas about the nature of society, it also directly violates some other articulated views—particularly some religious views. There are those who believe society was ordained by one or more supreme beings to turn out the way it has. These religiously deterministic views allow no room for human choices. Of course, there are other religious views holding that supreme beings have laid down principles humans should follow, but these latter views tend to give humans an agency by which to follow those principles or stray from them. This allows for periodic warnings that humans are going to hell in a hand basket. The autopoietic view of society requires no position for or against the idea of supremely ordained rules of life.

Here's a somewhat more limited example of autopoiesis in society: The World Wide Web. The Internet is a global network of computer servers that make a variety of communications possible. The web is what we have done with that possibility. Take a minute to reflect on the variety of content you are probably familiar with: e-mail, Google, Facebook, YouTube, Netflix, Twitter, Wikipedia, university websites, online banking, porno sites (well, you're probably not familiar with those), etc. The point is: nobody planned all that. The web is a self-creating entity, and it's an ongoing process. Every time some innovation appears on the web, it redefines what the web is and does. And that innovation changes the potential for future innovations. The web is clearly an autopoietic entity.

Potentially, the notion of autopoiesis can be a fundamental organizing principle for the study of society. However, at this writing, it is not seen as such. More's the pity.

3

Paradigms

The two preceding chapters have pointed to a certain tenuousness of knowledge. Nothing we know is safe from challenge,
modification, and even brutal destruction. Sometimes, knowledge
changes in bits and pieces. In this chapter, I look at the most basic
kind of change in our knowledge: change in the systems within
which we think.

A *paradigm* is a fundamental model or system for understanding things. The Ptolemaic model of the solar system mentioned
earlier is an example of a paradigm. In it, the sun revolved
around the earth, or revolved around points that revolved around
points that revolved around the earth. The Copernican system
that replaced Ptolemy's was another paradigm.

Geometry offers useful examples of paradigms and paradigm
shifts. Geometry was one of my favorite courses in high school,
and I did extremely well in it. As I've later learned, what I did
well in was Euclidean plane geometry. Parallel lines never met
this side of infinity, which was far enough away to be of no concern. The angles in a triangle always totaled 180 degrees; all lines
were straight.

Some brutal shocks were awaiting me in college, however.
For example, I soon discovered that there were a number of non-
Euclidean geometries that had truly bizarre rules. On the face of a
sphere, for example, perfectly straight lines met far short of infinity. Euclidean geometry is a paradigm, a model within which to
work. Unfortunately, at an early age I learned it as the *Truth* about
the way the world is. When I was later asked to shift to another
paradigm, I found the task difficult, if not insurmountable. The
shift of paradigms is not so much a shift in the particular things

35

we think as it is a shift in the systems we think within. By way of further illustration, here are some sociological paradigms.

The *interactionist* paradigm in sociology holds that human social life consists of interactions through which individuals create shared meanings. Life is like a hand of bridge in which your bid tells me something about the cards you hold, my bid communicates information about my cards to you, and eventually we arrive at a strategy for playing the hand.

The *social systems* or *structural/functional* paradigm treats society and social groups as integrated wholes composed of parts, with each part performing functions within the whole. From this perspective, life is like a symphony orchestra: some members play violins, some play horns, and one stands in front and directs.

Finally, the *conflict* paradigm regards social life as a struggle for domination. From this perspective, life is like a war—sometimes hot, sometimes cold—in which competing groups (social classes, religious groups, political parties) vie for supremacy over their opponents.

For some sociologists, these three paradigms are useful tools that can be brought to bear in examining social situations. None is better or truer than the others. In this sense, the paradigms are like a photographer's camera lenses. One lens may be useful for shots in the glaring sun, one for close-ups of small or distant objects, one for soft effects, and so on—though there is usually value in taking a look through each of them in every situation.

Sometimes, however, sociologists get attached to a particular paradigm. Devoted interactionists may have trouble seeing anything except interactions; functionalists may identify a function in everything; conflict theorists may find struggle everywhere they look. For some, their sociological paradigms spill over into all aspects of their lives.

Imagine three such sociologists selling furniture:

Interactionist: Buy this love seat so you and your honey can really get together.

Functionalist: Every home needs a spare bed for when friends stay over.

Conflict theorist: How about a king-size bed? Your neighbors just bought a queen-size bed.

Here they are planning a dinner party together:

Interactionist: How about fondue for an appetizer? That'll give everyone a chance to get together and chat.

Functionalist: Good idea. The cheese will provide lots of protein.

Conflict theorist: But some of our fondue forks are longer than others. People will fight for the longest forks.

Here's how they spent their spare time during college:

Interactionist: Cocktail parties

Functionalist: Computer programming

Conflict theorist: Debate team

What do you suppose would be the first things they would teach the family dog?

Interactionist: Shake hands

Functionalist: Fetch the paper

Conflict theorist: Bark at intruders

These examples indicate how paradigms affect what people see in the world around them. Here are some paradigms from daily life that you may see your world through, or at least recognize in people around you.

People who interpret the world through a system of fundamentalist Christian beliefs see many things around them as manifestations of the struggle between good and evil. Sex education in the schools is not merely a program they find unwise; it is the work of Satan. So is socialism. Similarly, some Marxists see their entire world as an expression of class struggle. If their pencil breaks, it is further evidence of greedy capitalists using substandard materials. Some people view all churches and all corporate contributions to charities as tax dodges. Yet other people see life in terms of market capitalism. Everything has a price, and people are under a natural obligation to amass as much wealth as they can and to look out for themselves.

I am not talking about simply holding certain beliefs or having certain values. Paradigms are more fundamental than that. Our paradigms organize our reality; they provide the most basic ground rules for dealing with life.

Perhaps you do not personally relate to any of the paradigms I've described so far, though you may know of people who seem to represent what I'm talking about. If that's the case, you have probably concluded that those people are in the wrong, that they are narrow-minded, prejudiced, and so forth. Now, I want to make things a little more uncomfortable.

You probably consider yourself a fairly rational and logical person. If you become irrational or illogical, you probably regret it later. You may have won arguments at times by showing that your opponent's position was illogical, or you may have lost arguments for being the illogical one. Underlying all this is *rationality* as a paradigm. Indeed rationality is so fundamental to your worldview that you may have a little trouble seeing it as a paradigm.

Consider how you react to the idea that rationality is a paradigm, not the method that reveals the ultimate truth of the universe. You may feel somewhat uncomfortable with the idea, asking yourself, "What's the alternative? Irrationality? I'll stick with rationality, thank you." If you do feel this way, you have an opportunity to learn something really important about paradigms. Take a minute to look at your thoughts and feelings to see what's making you uncomfortable. What's the nature of your commitment to rationality? What makes rationality so great, anyway? What would happen if you were to let go of your commitment to rationality? What would you have to lose? These are some of the questions that may assist you in focusing on your attachment to the paradigm of rationality.

If you have any attachment to rationality as a worldview, you probably imagine that giving up that attachment would leave you a blithering idiot, sitting in the corner babbling incoherently. You'd certainly be undependable and of no value to people around you; all your education would be wasted; chances are you'd be sent away to a hospital for people who've given up their commitment to rationality.

By now, you may have concluded that I am trying to talk you into being irrational. I may sound as though I am opposed to rationality. Let's look again.

There's another alternative to rationality other than irrationality. It is also possible to approach life *nonrationally*. Rather than being the opposite of rational, you can simply come to life in a way that's neither rational nor irrational. In fact, you already do that often in your life. Don't try to dance or make love rationally. If you think humor is rational, try to explain a joke to someone and see how much laughter you provoke. Or read a scholarly analysis of humor—not usually a barrel of chuckles. But such activities don't call for irrationality either. Love, your experience of music, art, and literature, and similar activities exist in a realm separate from rationality and irrationality.

None of this challenges the validity or value of rationality. Rationality is enormously useful. Try getting to the moon or building a bridge without it. It's a powerful paradigm. But it's only a paradigm, not the way things really are. Once you realize that, you will have multiplied the arrows in your quiver. Now you can choose the occasions when rationality is called for and those when it is not. You will be able to shift paradigms at will rather than being their victim.

If you actually succeed in stepping outside rationality in the way I've been describing, you will find an unexpected prize. Not only will you be able to add new dimensions to your approach to life, but you'll be better at using rationality. Rationality is a much more potent tool when you approach it from the outside rather than from inside.

I've elaborated on rationality because it is a particularly constraining paradigm for modern Americans and others, especially academics. As such, it gives you an opportunity to see the power of paradigms.

Here's a final example of a paradigm. There is a voice speaking to you from what seems like the back of your head. If you are a slow reader, that voice probably vocalizes everything for you. It also warns you to be on guard against people who are out to get you, tells you what to say to your date or mate, and is always there to point out your errors. It's the voice that says things like this:

"Nice going. You just told a dirty joke to a nun."

"You'd better think up a good excuse for not doing your homework."

"That guy just insulted you. You'd better do something."

The voice in my head is like a radio station. Sometimes when I'm shaving in the morning, it runs on and on like a news program. Other times, it dramatizes past and possible events in my life. In all these dramatizations, I am the clear winner. I always have just the right thing to say. If you don't know what I mean by the voice in the back of your head, stop reading for a minute and be very quiet. The voice in your head may be saying things like, "What is he talking about? I don't hear any voice. Boy, is this a weird book. Is it time to start reading again?" That's the voice I mean.

Evidence suggests that the ancient Greeks (and probably everyone before them) regarded that voice as divine. The voice said, "You must attack Troy!" and the ships were launched. When the voice said, "That man is going to attack you!" the body sprang into action.

Psychologist Julian Jaynes (1976) suggested that *consciousness* was born when people came to see that voice as being their own rather than a god's. That was certainly a powerful shift of paradigms.

But consider this further shift of paradigms regarding that voice talking from the back of your head. Some people argue that the voice is not the totality of who you are—that it's just a string of chatter emanating from your past experiences and from recesses of your mind. In this new paradigm, the voice in the back of your head isn't necessarily accurate in its commentary on your life. Let's say your best friend passes you on the street without speaking. Your voice says, "She hates me." It may very well be that your friend simply didn't see you. At the very least you are not required to abide by the opinions and instructions coming from the voice. If the voice says, "Fight!" you can still walk on by if you choose.

As in the example of rationality, this new paradigm actually expands your possibilities. You still have your voice. You can listen to it, take charge of it when you want, give it topics to discuss, step in and change the flow of chatter. None of this would be possible, however, if you thought you *were* that voice.

These comments are all intended to draw your attention to the power of paradigms. The most potent moments of science are those when paradigms shift. These shifts can be more powerful than shifts of tectonic plates that send seismic waves around the world, generating earthquakes and volcanic eruptions. After an earthquake, people can eventually get back to business as usual, but that's not possible after a paradigm shift.

Paradigm shifts are extremely difficult—on both sides of the street. They are difficult to cause and difficult to comprehend. The problem is that each of us listens through our paradigms. When we hear something new and strange, we try desperately to fit it into the old and familiar. When I began describing rationality as only a paradigm, for example, you may have heard it through a paradigm that only allowed rationality and irrationality—omitting the possibility of nonrationality.

You'd do well to empathize with the sixteenth-century scientists who had so much trouble conceiving what Copernicus had to say, or with twentieth-century scientists who first tried to understand Einsteinian relativity using Newtonian minds. There is no easy solution to the constraints that paradigms place on us. Ultimately, humility is probably the healthiest quality to bring to new ideas. The arrogance of certainty is a constant impediment to science, social and otherwise. Growing is more important than knowing.

So far, I've been talking mostly about the troublesome nature of paradigms, and I want to bring matters into balance now. While paradigms can conceal things from us, they can also reveal things we wouldn't have seen otherwise. In recent years, I have been particularly interested in the subject of individuals' taking personal responsibility for public problems: everything from litter and traffic congestion through crime in the streets and prejudice to world hunger and global climate change. Although we often feel powerless to affect such problems, sometimes we step forward and take action.

Thus, for example, Martin Luther King, Jr., assumed personal responsibility for correcting the problems of race relations in America; Ralph Nader stepped forward to establish the groundwork for consumer rights; Paul Ehrlich took responsibility for the problem of overpopulation; Al Gore took responsibility for drawing attention to climate change. None of these people took *sole* responsibility, but they made the problems they saw as their *personal* responsibility. Less dramatically, a man steps into the street to pick up a broken bottle before someone runs over it and gets a flat tire; a young woman, concerned about a stop sign that has been knocked down near her house, digs out the hole, replants the sign, and tamps down the dirt.

Initially, I asked, "Why do some people take responsibility for public problems?" or "Why do all of us take responsibility sometimes?" The more I studied the matter, however, the more I became convinced that all or most of us *want* to make a difference in the ways I've just described. Both in my own experience and in what others told me, it became clear that taking personal responsibility for public problems is a source of profound satisfaction. Typical, perhaps, was the student who swept some broken glass off a highway and reported, "I looked back at the road afterward and had the distinct feeling that it belonged to me. I'd do it again." Eventually, my research question became, "Why *don't* people take responsibility for public problems?" The three sociological paradigms mentioned earlier in this chapter have all been very useful in pursuing that question.

The social systems paradigm, for example, has highlighted the impact of specialization on responsibility within a modern, complex society. Many of the social problems that interest me have been made the official responsibility of particular individuals and agencies. Thus, the young woman who repaired the stop sign near her house was doing the work of the city streets department.

A few years ago a student in my social problems course was walking through a public park and noticed a bunch of beer bottles scattered on the ground near a trash can. He decided this offered a good opportunity to test the notion of taking personal responsibility, so he began picking up the bottles and putting them in the trash can. Before he realized it, a police squad car pulled up beside him and two officers got out. The following conversation ensued.

"What are you doing?"

"I'm picking up these beer bottles."

"Don't you know you aren't supposed to drink beer in the park?"

"I didn't drink the beer. I'm just picking up the bottles."

My student reports that the officers simply stood there for a few moments, trying to cope with what he had told them. Finally, one of them said, "Why don't you just move along. We have a parks crew that takes care of that." Clearly, they couldn't make sense out of his cleaning up a public mess he hadn't created. Probably they thought he had lied about drinking the beer. Maybe they thought he was stealing trash.

The social systems paradigm has also been useful in encouraging people to take personal responsibility for public problems. Where a particular problem falls within the official responsibility of some public agency, private individuals can sometimes solve the problem by getting the public officials to do their duty. For example, the young woman I mentioned could have reported the fallen stop sign to the streets department and kept calling until they did something about it.

The conflict paradigm has illuminated other aspects of the matter. Often, individuals refuse to take personal responsibility because they feel they would be allowing others to dominate them. People who feel they are in a constant struggle with the government, say, are not likely to spend their own time and energy doing work they feel ought to be accomplished by tax dollars. Others refrain from taking action if they feel large corporations, churches, labor unions, or welfare recipients are to blame for the problem. As a general rule, the conflict paradigm points out the link most people make between responsibility and blame. Like the social systems paradigm, the conflict perspective can be wielded by people who want to make a difference—in bringing pressure to bear on public officials, for example, or in building effective coalitions or coping with the power plays of others.

The interactionist perspective has revealed still other aspects of the issue. In particular, I have seen the influence on our actions of what we believe others will think about us when we act responsibly. Suppose you and I are walking along the highway, and we come upon a tree branch that has fallen onto the road, blocking one of the lanes. Cars are backed up, waiting for a clear lane so they can drive around the branch. As we are passing by, I go out to the road, grab the branch, and pull it out of the way. Chances are, you may think that's a little unusual. Perhaps you'll feel a little guilty that you didn't do it; I seem like a more responsible citizen than you. If you have that thought, you may rationalize it away by telling yourself I was just showing off. You may even think that I was trying to be self-righteous or "holier than thou." Even if you don't think any of those things, I'm likely to think you are thinking them.

If you were the one to move the branch, there's a possibility that I would think those things about you. I'm certainly more likely to feel guilty, since I'm the one who's been talking about taking personal responsibility for public problems. Now you've made me look as though it were all talk and no action. You've really put me down. You were obviously looking for an opportunity to make me look bad. Even if I don't think any of those things, you're likely to think I'm thinking them.

The interactionist perspective has also drawn attention to another side to all this. Sometimes when one person acts responsibly, others join in. Start picking up trash in a public park or at the beach and you may find others begin doing the same. In the face of a prevailing agreement not to take on public problems, it is sometimes possible to trigger a movement in the other direction.

These are but a few illustrations of the ways in which the three paradigms have illuminated different aspects of individuals taking personal responsibility for public problems. None of the paradigms provides a complete or true picture. All paradigms ever give us are partial views of things, but those partial views can be powerful and useful nonetheless.

Take a moment to reflect on some of the different paradigms associated with each of the following hot topics. Don't stop with differences in attitudes and beliefs but see if you can identify the implicit, unexamined frameworks that condition views on different sides of the debates.

- Abortion
- Gay Marriage

- Voting Rights
- Immigration
- Race Relations
- Marijuana

While we've all heard a variety of opinions expressed in connection with these topics, it is useful to look behind the opinions to see the fundamental points of view, or points from which to view, that give rise to those opinions.

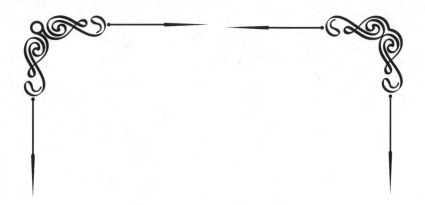

PART 2

THE STRUCTURING
OF INQUIRY

4

Determinism versus Freedom

In this chapter I take up one of the most sensitive issues of social research—so sensitive, in fact, that it is almost never discussed. Whenever I asked colleagues to suggest ways I might improve *The Practice of Social Research*, in fact, this is the topic they most often suggested dropping. (So I did, and this is where it landed.)

Determinism is an embarrassment for social scientists. It is a fundamental paradigm for nearly all of our research, yet none of us wants to speak out on its behalf. Closer to the bone, our livelihoods depend on determinism, and yet we hope it isn't true. Crudely put, social research assumes a deterministic paradigm that fundamentally denies the existence of free will. Here's an example of how it works.

A standard research question for social researchers would be something like, "What causes prejudice?" Most people would recognize this as a worthwhile subject for research: if we knew what caused prejudice, we might be able to eliminate it.

Millions of dollars have been invested in research aimed at discovering various aspects of what causes prejudice, and a great deal has been learned. For example, prejudice and education are largely incompatible; fundamentalist Christian beliefs seem to promote anti-Semitism; associating with minority-group members tends to reduce prejudice toward them. In fact, laws that make discrimination illegal seem to have the long-term effect of reducing prejudice, suggesting that you can legislate morality. But every time we discover that prejudice (or tolerance) is *caused* by something, we drive another nail in the coffin of individual choice and freedom. To see what I mean, imagine the following research report.

We've studied prejudice exhaustively, and we conclude that some people are prejudiced because they want to be and others aren't prejudiced because they don't want to be.

A researcher submitting that report would not continue to receive funding very long. When we ask for reasons for prejudice, we expect reasons. How can you prevent prejudice if you don't know what causes it?

Here's the rub. If people's prejudice is caused by such things as their level of education, their religion, and where they grew up, they didn't have anything to say about it. They were the victims of circumstances beyond their control. It's as though they were machines or robots, not human beings exercising free will. We don't normally put the matter quite so crudely, but that's the implication of the model social science is based on.

Notice the implications of this model for crime and punishment. If I robbed the bank because of social forces beyond my control, is it really appropriate to punish me? Don't the forces that are controlling me constitute "extenuating circumstances?" If someone stuck a gun to my head and made me cooperate in a bank robbery, you probably wouldn't think I should be punished. This argument has been an important theme in the American criminal justice system in recent decades, in part because researchers have been able to explain criminal behavior on the basis of social determinism. What I've said about prejudice and crime applies equally to all other human characteristics—to tolerance as much as to prejudice, for example. Observing that some people are more religious than others, social researchers seek to find the factors responsible. There's no room in the model for people simply choosing to be religious.

What's your political preference? Republican? Democrat? Independent? Whatever it is, you probably feel that you made a personal and well-reasoned choice. But social researchers assume that your choice was made for you by factors beyond your control, and they're pretty effective at finding out what those factors are. In the end, this model implicitly assumes that everything you are and do is determined by forces you cannot control and may not be aware of. The implication is that you have no freedom.

Be clear that I am not saying you *are* totally determined, but that's the clear implication of the model on which explanatory science is based. Whenever we look for causes, we imply that we are caused.

This basic model is the same one used in the natural sciences. When we boil a pot of water, we say that the heat causes the water to turn to steam. We never ask whether the water chose to become steam any more than we ask whether a rock wants to fall when we throw it off a cliff. Gravity causes the rock to fall.

The model is more threatening when we apply it to human beings, although there are some limits to this. We don't mind saying that a virus causes us to cough and have a runny nose or that a bump on the head causes us to lose consciousness. We don't protest our loss of freedom in situations like those.

Sometimes we are willing to let external social forces cause our failures in life. We may blame losing our jobs on the economy, greedy bosses, or cheap foreign labor. We hold our spouses to be the cause of our unhappy marriages. Still, we are unwilling to consider ourselves to be totally determined. Let's see why.

For one thing, the idea of being totally determined contradicts our experience of life. The deterministic model suggests that whether you go to college and how well you do in your studies are caused by forces beyond your control. And yet you have the experience of deciding whether to go to college. You do whatever is necessary to get admitted. Once enrolled, you study, do your assignments, and generally feel responsible for how it all turns out. If someone were to tell you that your success in college was actually being determined by forces beyond your control, you might laugh at the notion. Your good grades were caused by your hard work, and you decided to study rather than to go to the movies. Right?

Don't answer too quickly. Social research confirms that studying is an important factor in the determination of grades, but let's look a little more deeply into who decided you should study hard. Let's assume you're the student in question, and I'll try to discover who's really responsible for your good grades.

Me: Why did you get good grades?

You: Because I studied hard.

Me: Okay. Why did you study hard?

You: Because I wanted to get good grades.

Me: Makes sense. Why did you want to get good grades?

You: What do you mean? Everybody wants to get good grades.

Me: Maybe, but if everyone wanted good grades as much as you did, then they all would have studied as hard as you, and they all would have gotten good grades.

You: Okay, so maybe I wanted good grades more than other students. In part, I knew it would mean a lot to my family. Just about everyone in our family has gone to college for generations—and most of them seem to have done well.

Me: I understand.

You: But there's more to it than that. Both my parents are physicians, running a medical clinic together. For as long as I can remember, they have talked about me going to medical school and then joining them in their practice. It would break their hearts if I didn't do well in college and couldn't get into medical school.

Me: As I listen to what you say, it sounds more and more to me as though your good grades were not the result of your free choice. Consider this. A student comes from a family in which just about everyone had gone to college for generations and had gotten good grades. The student's parents are both physicians and have always wanted their child to attend medical school and join them in their practice. I'd wager that just about anyone with that background would study hard and do well.

You: Well, those circumstances have obviously had something to do with my studying hard, but that's not the whole story. It was still my choice. I didn't have to study. I could have goofed off.

Me: I'm not so sure.

You: Okay, here's proof. I have an older brother who obviously had the same background as me in the ways we've discussed, and I know my parents wanted him to join them in the practice. However, he spent all his time in college partying and he flunked out. So that disproves the argument that free choice doesn't matter.

Me: Perhaps. If that's the case, let's find out more about how your free choice operated in the matter. Why do you suppose you make your free choice to study whereas your brother didn't? Why did your brother make a free choice to spend his time partying rather than studying?

You: Well, I've always had the feeling that my parents pushed him too hard. I think his failure in college was his way of resisting their pressure. It's ironic that this comes up in our discussion of determinism and free choice. I guess he felt our parents were trying to determine his future, and he wanted to prove he had a choice in the matter.

Me: And if your parents had pushed you like that, do you think you might have goofed off and flunked out?

You: I think there would be a good chance of that.

Me: So the reason for your success and your brother's failure is that your parents pushed him too hard but didn't do that to you. I'm not sure I see where your free choice was in that. In fact, it sounds a little like your brother's attempt to show he had free choice was actually caused by your parents' pressure.

You: Well, maybe that's a bad example. Besides, we've only scratched the surface of why I got good grades. For example, you yourself said that studying hard had some impact on grades. But that's not the whole picture. I didn't want to say this before, but I'm simply smarter than my brother.

Me: Is that something you chose, or is it more of your circumstances?

This discussion could continue almost endlessly, but the end result would be the same. Every time I asked you for a reason why you got good grades, you'd have one. The problem is that you are trapped by your reasons. Every reason you give for your good grades takes away from your free choice in the matter. Even when the reason looks like an example of free choice (studying hard, for example), that reason turns out to have reasons behind it that undermine your freedom.

If this point is not clear to you, try the following exercise.

1. Select some action you've taken or some characteristic that describes you.

2. Write down the 10 most important reasons why you took that action or have that characteristic.

3. For each of those 10 reasons, write the 5 most important reasons why those first-level reasons are true for you.

4. Now write the 3 most important reasons why each of the 50 second-level reasons is true for you.

5. Now ask yourself how likely it is that anyone with those 210 reasons would have taken the action or had the characteristic you started the exercise with.

6. If you can honestly say that someone with all those reasons might have turned out differently, ask yourself how that could possibly be. The reason you now give should be added to your list of reasons. Now repeat this step.

There's simply no way out. The paradigm we operate within demands this outcome. And remember, the same paradigm is used by social researchers studying human behavior.

If you find this discussion disconcerting, you should take a moment to consider why you are reading this book. The deterministic model suggests that you have to be reading it right now. I certainly can't know all the reasons that forced you to be reading the book, but I can guess at some. Perhaps you've been assigned the book for a college course. Perhaps a close friend urged you to read it, and you feel you owe it to that friendship to read the book. Perhaps you've gotten hooked by the discussion, and you can't put it down until you know how it turns out. Whatever your reasons, the deterministic model suggests that you have no choice but to be reading this book right now.

Before you assert your independence by closing the book, consider two more points. First, if you stop reading the book right now, the deterministic model suggests that you were forced to do so. Perhaps your discomfort made you quit. Maybe it was something I said. If you had to quit because you were late for class, that's a perfect example of your quitting having been determined.

Second, no matter what you do, I'll still be here saying these things about determinism, social science, and freedom. You can slam the book shut, chop it up into little pieces, and burn the shredded paper. Then, twenty years from now, you'll be in a used-book store and see a worn out, dog-eared copy of this book. You'll pick it up, open to this page, and I'll still be here saying the same things. Worse yet, I'll know that you've come back to the book, just as I know you're reading now. (Realize that if you quit reading, you'll never know if I think you're still reading. You'll have to peek back in here to find out and Zap!—I'll get you again. You're hopelessly trapped. I'm like the light inside your refrigerator.)

The real problem we have with the deterministic model, I think, lies not so much in what it says about our past and present as in what it says about our future. Just as the model says you didn't have any freedom in the past, it also says you have none from now on. In fact, the model suggests that how you turn out, whether you will succeed or fail in various ventures, whether you will be basically satisfied or dissatisfied during the remainder of your life, is already determined. Given the trillions of pieces making up your current circumstances, what happens in your life seems inevitable, and you seem to lack the freedom to change them. That's the implication of the model.

It's worth noting that millions of people around the world accept fatalistic world views essentially like this. Many Muslims, for example, consider life merely the unfolding of Allah's will and consider themselves merely players in the predetermined drama.

In talking to hundreds of students about this topic, I have found that their greatest discomfort about determinism involves fears about what they would be like if they accepted it as true. Let's resume our previous fictitious dialogue and look at some of those fears.

Me: So how do you think you'd behave if you accepted the notion that you have no free choice?

You: I'd simply give up. Why on earth should I study hard and try to get good grades if I really believed that I had no control over how things would turn out? Do you think I'd keep trying to be a good student?

Me: Okay, so you're afraid that you might quit school if you accepted a totally deterministic image of human life. How else would you behave?

You: It's not just a matter of quitting school, damn it! I mean really quit: just drop out, stop caring about anything. Like, for example, I spend a lot of time and energy working for social justice. I see a lot of things around me that just aren't right, and I devote a lot of myself to making them better. Now, do you think I'd keep working for social justice if I really believed that my every thought, word, and deed—not to mention the future of the world—was already determined, that I couldn't really change anything? Do you think I'd even care? Do you think anyone would, if they believed that? If I believed in determinism, I would be a totally different person. Do you understand what I am saying?

Me: I understand that you are concerned that you'd be a different kind of person if you accepted that you were totally determined, but I want to hear some more about how you'd change.

You: I've already told you. I wouldn't care about things that mean a lot to me now. I'd stop trying to make a contribution to causes that mean a lot to me. I wouldn't try to get ahead.

Me: I appreciate your concerns that you might give up trying to succeed personally and might give up trying to make a difference in the world, but my question is this: how would you change if you truly accepted a totally deterministic view of life?

You: I've told you! I'd change totally. I'd become a totally different person. It wouldn't be a pretty sight. I'd just sit in a corner and not do anything. Or maybe I'd watch television all day and night. No. I know what. I'd just devote myself to having a good time. I wouldn't care about the future since it's already taken care of. Right?

Me: Again, I hear the fears you have about what you might be like, but I still want to know how you'd change if you truly accepted a totally deterministic view of life.

You: There you go again. I've already told you how I'd change.

Me: You've told me what you might look like afterward. I want to know how you'd change.

You: But I told you how I'd change. . . . Wait a minute. When you say how, do you mean, like, how?

Me: That's it exactly.

You: You mean if I truly accepted the view that everything I think, say, do, and am is totally caused by forces over which I have no personal control, how would I change? How could I?

Me: And what would you be like if you accepted that view?

You: Well, if life really was totally determined, and I came from a family who all went to college and wanted me to join their medical practice, I guess I'd study hard and get good grades.

Me: Would you feel bad about things being that way?

You: Not unless I was determined to feel bad.

You and I are so deeply embedded in the view that we have free choice that our greatest fears about determinism refer to the irresponsible free choices we think we'd make if we found out we didn't have any freedom. Ironic, isn't it? If it turned out that you didn't have any freedom, you couldn't make any free choices—irresponsible or otherwise.

We don't know whether you have free choice or are completely determined, but we do know that whichever is the case, you aren't going to change things. So you can probably find better things to do with your time and energy than worry about whether or not you have free choice.

Before leaving our examination of determinism, let's consider two additional aspects of the issue. First, let's take a closer look at what a deterministic world would be like. I think you may be surprised by what you find.

Consider a world in which everything you do, think, and feel is a product of the multitude of forces, events, and circumstances that bear on you. Why did you go to the movies last night, for example? (If you didn't go last night, recall the last time you did go to the movies.) Perhaps your friend pressured you into it. Or maybe it was a chance to be with him or her. Maybe you were bored with everything else. Maybe you felt like celebrating something. Or maybe you've always wanted to see *Texas Chainsaw Massacre* and this was the last night it was showing. If you're honest about it, you must admit that you had reasons for going.

However, your going to the movies was also the product of forces and factors you are less conscious of. For example, you couldn't have gone if someone hadn't written the script for the movie, if someone else hadn't directed it, if others hadn't performed in it, if others hadn't run cameras, and so forth. Nor could you have gone if someone hadn't decided to build the theater you attended, to book the movie, and to advertise it online so you knew about it. Come to think of it, your going to that movie also depended on somebody inventing the Internet (not to mention chainsaws).

The weather probably had an influence. If you drove to the theater, everything involved in your having that car (as well as the invention, development, and marketing of automobiles) cannot be discounted in explaining how you came to be at the movies. For your life to have turned out exactly as it did when you arrived at the movies, it was necessary for everything that preceded that moment to have happened exactly as it did. If any tiny piece of the past had been different, your life would have turned out somewhat differently, and you might never have made it to the movies.

Garrett Hardin, the ecologist, has said the first rule of ecology is that "you can't do just one thing." Everything is related to everything else, and everything has some influence on everything else. (This is the theme of the movie, *The Butterfly Effect*.) Thus, your being at the movies that night, as well as the state of mind you brought to the theater, was in some degree a consequence of, say, how your parents felt about movies. Moreover, how they felt about the movies had its own complex and lengthy string of causes.

Newtonian physicists shared a notion that all the empty space around them was filled with ether: invisible, odorless, but capable of transmitting electromagnetic waves. Ether was postulated because the physicists believed that all waves needed a medium to pass through (air is needed for sound waves), and yet light waves were able to pass through a vacuum. Ether was the explanation of choice until Einstein's theory of relativity eliminated the need for a medium. Physicists no longer believe in ether, but I think it's a useful image for our present discussion. Imagine that ether pervades every nook and cranny of your life, that you swim through life in an ocean of ether, and that ether is made up of all the reasons and causes that affect your thoughts, feelings, and behavior.

Everything that happens on the planet affects you in some way. Someone in China sneezes, and somehow, to some tiny degree, that sneeze reverberates through the ether and has an impact on whether you go to the movies, whether you study hard, whether you marry the person of your dreams. This means that everything you do, think, and feel is a product of trillions of unknown and unseen events around the world.

If you truly sense what I am describing, you may feel trapped by all those forces. Clearly you have no freedom in the matter. Everything you do, think, or feel can be explained in terms of external forces. And the internal causes you may fall back on ("I went to the movies because I wanted to") get explained away in short order ("Why did you want to go?" "Because my friends said it was good").

A physical model that would accurately represent the model of the universe I've been describing might consist of a tabletop model of some pastoral setting with trees, farmers, cows, field mice, hay, clouds, birds, tractors, and so forth. All the parts of this model would move in manners similar to their real-life counterparts. The birds would fly, and the trees would grow out of the ground to maturity, fall to earth, and be replaced by new trees. All these moving parts would be mechanically connected to each other in a manner that simulated the causal interrelationships connecting things in the real world. If one part were moved, the others would move too.

Such a model would serve as an excellent teaching device for elementary school courses in ecology. "See how the bird guano makes the grass grow for the cows to eat so they can produce milk to make the farmer strong enough to drive the tractor and plow the fields and plant seeds that the birds eat?"

The main point of the model, however, would be achieved when some young child suddenly realized that it didn't matter which part was moved—with no slack in the system, when one part was moved, all the others would move simultaneously, like gears fit tightly together. If the child were young enough and naive enough, he or she might be able to explain the ultimate logic of cause and effect to all the rest of us who already know too much.

Suppose for the moment that we do live in an absolutely deterministic world. Suppose there is absolutely no slack in the system. One part moves and all the others move accordingly, without fail. If that's the nature of the world system you live in, you are either totally the effect of all those other parts or you are the total cause. You go to the movies and someone in China sneezes.

Here's a less fanciful example to make the same point. Imagine a police officer chasing a thief down an alley. Who is the cause and who the effect? Is the police officer's pursuit causing the thief's flight or is it the other way around? Now imagine that the alley ends abruptly; the officer's gun is drawn; the thief is apprehended. "Hands up!" the officer shouts. The thief's hands go up a little. "Higher!" Up a little more. "Higher!" Once again, we see officer and thief intertwined in a dance in which it's not clear who's leading whom.

Students often are bothered by the deterministic element in social research, since it seems to deny their personal freedom. It's important, therefore, to realize that the system they fear is in fact a paradoxical one. You can't totally lose your freedom without simultaneously having more power than you ever imagined.

As I've said earlier, no one knows the truth about whether or not this is a deterministic world. Few of us seem to live our lives as though we felt it was totally deterministic, but to the extent that we do regard it as being so, we are as much cause as effect.

Social scientific explanation is based on a deterministic model. So far, it has been a useful model. We've learned a lot about how and why people are the ways they are, and we can often predict what people will do. Thus it makes no sense to resist the social scientific use of this model.

The final point I want to make concerns the model per se. As indicated earlier, social scientists tend to employ the deterministic model implicitly but seldom discuss or examine it explicitly. I think this causes us to lose an important opportunity. While we usually regard determinism as an embarrassing constant, it is at least possible that it is really a variable. Some people may be more determined than others, for example, or more determined in some aspects than they are in others.

Consider people's food preferences. What we like or dislike in the way of food can be pretty powerful in our lives. Sometimes we spend hours preparing (or much money buying) a particular dish that we love. At the other end of the scale, just the thought of some kinds of food can make us ill. Imagine eating rotting alligator carcass—raw. If the thought doesn't make you a little queasy, I'll bet the real thing would put you under the table.

Many of our food preferences and aversions, moreover, are clearly determined by our culture and socialization. For many Americans, the thought of eating raw fish is only a short distance from the thought of eating rotting alligator carcass, whereas sashimi has long been a delicacy for Japanese (and is becoming one for growing numbers of Americans). Some Americans would have the same negative reaction to the idea of eating snails, but of course, the French love escargot.

While many of our food preferences and aversions are determined, we do change over time. We may even learn to like broccoli and lose interest in candy. If you look at your own experience in this regard, you'll probably feel that some of your preferences are pretty rigidly entrenched (you're not touching rotting alligator carcass, no matter what) while others are more flexible (you might be willing to try rattlesnake or even monkey brains).

As a practical matter, at least, our food preferences and aversions seem not to be equally determined; it might make sense to see determinism as a variable in this respect. Moreover, you probably know someone who is far more rigid about food than you are, and you probably know someone else who is more willing than you to try strange things. Thus, determinism may vary across people as well as across specific situations for a single person.

Apart from the issue of food, you have certain beliefs, attitudes, and interests that are more firmly entrenched than others. Your belief (or disbelief or nonbelief) in God may or may not be stronger than your choice of a favorite professional football team. Some people consider their jobs more important than their families; for others it's the other way around. Some people would choose death before dishonor; others wouldn't. Some people's nationality is so important to them that they are willing to go to war and kill people of other nations; others will kill for religion; still others will kill on the basis of language differences.

All these examples illustrate how such things as beliefs, attitudes, and interests can have a deterministic power over people—and how other people are not so determined. It seems possible to me that these are not random variations but that some people are generally less determined than others. If determinism is a variable, that would be worth knowing. We can never know it, however, unless we are willing to face the issue of determinism nose-to-nose and take our chances on how it all turns out.

Before leaving this examination, I'd like you to consider how problematic the concept of freedom is in its own right. For Americans and many others, freedom is a sacred value. "What do we want?" "Freedom!" "When do we want it?" "Now!" "Free at last, free at last, thank God Almighty we are free at last." Countless millions have suffered and died to achieve and protect freedom.

Seymour Martin Lipset (1963) pointed out that the two foundations of American democracy are freedom and equality. American politicians love to proclaim their undying commitment to these fundamental values. However, as Lipset also pointed out, these two values are incompatible. Freedom means the opportunity to do better than other people—to be unequal. Though they may both hate to admit it, the Democratic Party is the custodian of the equality value and the Republican Party is the custodian of freedom (Liberty).

Some examples of Democratic Party positions aimed at supporting equality would include such things as minimum wage, Social Security, progressive income taxes, and equal rights for women and minorities, to name just a few. Republicans, on the other hand, pursue the value of freedom with such aims as repeal of the estate tax on the wealthy, reducing capital gains taxes, and reducing regulations on businesses, among others. This is especially true of Republicans with a Libertarian bent, but some Republicans draw a line that withholds freedom as regards such things as abortion, marijuana, and sexual orientation.

The Democratic emphasis is based, in part, on a belief that much of our individual success or failure in mass society is a function of forces and factors beyond our control. People may lose their jobs because the factory where they work shuts down or moves to a Third World country. They may be unable to get work due to an overall economic recession—none of which is their responsibility. Notice this view is similar to the social science approach to human behavior, and it is no surprise that social scientists tend to be more liberal than the general population. In terms of social policy, if people cannot be held completely responsible for the disadvantages of poverty, unemployment, sickness, or growing old, it makes sense that the society at large—i.e., the government—should help alleviate their problems. Thus, Democrats are more likely to support programs like Social Security, Medicare, unemployment insurance, and the like.

The Republican commitment to protecting freedom is linked to a belief that individuals can achieve success if they simply work hard enough. They would not deny that some individuals may have a bigger challenge than others, but they are quick to point to people who have overcome enormous obstacles to succeed. To be sure, any Republican will acknowledge that some tragic cases warrant a helping hand, just as Democrats will acknowledge that some individual failure is grounded in laziness. Although this represents a fundamental difference in the two political outlooks, they differ in a matter of emphasis, not in commitments to absolutes.

I've paid a fair amount of attention to the question of free will and determinism over the years, not as scholars examine these issues, but as they show up in the lives of ordinary people. One of life's most common ironies is the denial of freedom by people who insist they act on that freedom. Raise the possibility that someone is totally determined in their behavior, and they vehemently deny it. Yet that same person will deny their freedom repeatedly all through the day. To illustrate, I suggest that my students listen to themselves.

"Want to go to the movies?"

"I can't. I have to study."

No, you don't. You don't have to study at all. You could go to the movies all the time—and watch TV when the theaters are closed. You could, but when you choose not to do so, you refuse to take the rap. You blame life's circumstances.

"I couldn't date a boy who smoked."

Sure you could. You could date a boy who smoked cigars, ate flies, and farted. You could do that even if you are a boy. You might choose not to do so, but chances are that you'll deny you had a choice in the matter.

"I couldn't tell my mother that."

Sure you could. You could tell her anything. You could tell her you smoke cigars, eat flies, and . . .

"No! That would kill her!"

You could tell her something that would kill her. I'm hoping you won't kill her, and I imagine she would share that hope. But when you choose not to tell her something that would kill her, why not take credit for that choice?

For all the times I have had conversations like this with students, I don't know that anyone has been lastingly affected by it. Most of us are mostly wired to deny our freedom most of the time. And I'm no different from you, most of the time.

Consider "falling in love." Nobody in the history of the human race has ever chosen to be in love. You can wish for it, look for it, wait for it, but ultimately it just happens to you. It's like catching the flu or mono or falling down a flight of stairs.

The anthem for this fundamental human orientation, which I usually sing to my audience, but which you'll be spared, goes something like this:

> You made me love you
> I didn't want to do it
> I didn't want to do it
> You made me love you
> And all the time you knew it
>
> (lyrics by Joseph McCarthy, 1913)

I invite you to listen to yourself and others through the rest of the day and see if you find examples of freedom being denied in the ways we communicate about our choices and actions. My clearest conclusion is that we are not clear on the matter of freedom.

5

———·ᘜᗯᕯᗯᘜᗯᕯ·———

Concepts, Indicators, and Reality

Measurement is one of the fundamental aspects of social research. When we describe science as logical/empirical, we mean that scientific conclusions should (1) make sense and (2) correspond to what we can observe. It is the second of these characteristics I explore in this essay.

Suppose we are interested in learning whether education really reduces prejudice. To do that, we must be able to measure both prejudice and education. Once we've distinguished prejudiced people from unprejudiced people and educated people from uneducated people, we'll be in a position to find out whether the two variables are related.

Social scientific measurement operates in accordance with the following implicit model:

- Prejudice exists as a *variable:* some people are more prejudiced than others.

- There are numerous *indicators* of prejudice.

- None of the indicators provides a perfect reflection of prejudice as it "really" is, but they can point to it at least approximately.

- We should try to find better and better indicators of prejudice—indicators that come ever closer to the "real thing."

This model applies to all of the variables social scientists study. Take a minute to look through the following list of variables commonly examined in social research.

arms race	alienation	education
religiosity	social class	liberalism
urbanism	age	authoritarianism
tv watching	self-esteem	race
susceptibility	idealism	happiness
stereotyping	prestige	powerlessness
anti-Semitism	tolerance	mobility
voting	fascism	consistency
dissonance	parochialism	delinquency
pessimism	maturity	compassion
anxiety	solidarity	democracy
revolution	instability	influence

Even if you've never taken a course in social science, many of these terms are at least somewhat familiar to you. Social scientists study things that are of general interest to everyone. Racism and stereotyping affect us all, for example, and they are special concerns for many of us. Differences in *religiosity* (some of us are more religious than others) are also of special interest to some people. As our country has evolved from small towns to large cities, we've all thought and talked more about *urbanism*—the good and bad associated with city life. Similar interests can be identified for all of the other terms.

My point is that you've probably thought about many of the variables mentioned in the list. Those you are familiar with undoubtedly have the quality of reality for you: that is, you know they exist. Religiosity, for example, is real. Regardless of whether you're in favor of it, opposed to it, or don't care much one way or the other, you at least know that religiosity exists. Or does it?

This is a particularly interesting question for me, since my first book, *To Comfort and to Challenge* (with Charles Glock and Benjamin Ringer), was about this subject. In particular, we wanted to know why some people were more religious than others (the sources of religiosity) and what impact differences in religiosity had on other aspects of life (the consequences of religiosity). Looking for the sources and consequences of a particular variable is a conventional social scientific undertaking; the first step is to develop a measure of that variable. We had to develop methods for distinguishing religious people, nonreligious people, and those somewhere in between.

The question we faced was: If religiosity is real, how do we know that? How do we distinguish religious people from nonreligious people? For most contemporary Americans, a number of answers come readily to mind. Religious people go to church, for example. They believe in the tenets of their faith. They pray. They read religious materials, such as the Bible, and they participate in religious organizations.

Not all religious people do all of these things, of course, and a great deal depends on their particular religious affiliation, if any. Christians believe in the divinity of Jesus; Jews do not. Muslims believe Mohammed's teachings are sacred; Jews and Christians do not. Some signs of religiosity are to be found in seemingly secular realms. Orthodox Jews, for example, refrain from eating pork; Seventh-Day Adventists don't drink alcohol.

In our study, we were interested in religiosity among a very specific group: Episcopal Church members in America. To simplify our present discussion, let's look at that much narrower question: How can you distinguish religious from nonreligious Episcopalians in America?

As I've indicated above, we are likely to say that religious people attend church, whereas nonreligious people do not. Thus, if we know someone who attends church every week, we're likely to think of that person as religious; indeed, religious people joke about church members who only attend services on Easter and at Christmas. The latter are presumed to be less religious.

Of course, we are speaking rather casually here, so let's see whether church attendance would be an adequate measure of religiosity for Episcopalians and other mainstream American Christians. Would you be willing to equate religiosity with church attendance? That is, would you be willing to call religious everyone who attended church every week, let's say, and call nonreligious everyone who did not?

I suspect that you would not consider equating church attendance with religiosity a wise policy. For example, consider a political figure who attends church every Sunday, sits in the front pew, puts a large contribution in the collection plate with a flourish, and by all other evidence seems only interested in being known as a religious person for the political advantage that may entail. Let's add that the politician in question regularly lies and cheats, exhibits no Christian compassion toward others, and ridicules religion in private. You'd probably consider it inappropriate to classify that person as religious.

Now imagine someone confined to a hospital bed, who spends every waking minute reading the Bible, leading other patients in prayer, raising money for missionary work abroad—but never going to church. Probably this would fit your image of a religious person.

These deviant cases illustrate that, while church attendance is somehow related to religiosity, it is not a sufficient indicator in and of itself. So how can we distinguish religious from nonreligious people?

Prayer is a possibility. Presumably, people who pray a lot are more religious than those who don't. But wouldn't it matter what they prayed for? Suppose they were only praying for money. How about the Muslim extremist praying daily for the extermination of the Jews? How about the athlete praying for an opponent to be hit by a truck? Like church attendance, prayer seems to have something to do with religiosity, but we can't simply equate the two.

We might consider religious beliefs. Among Christians, for example, it would seem to make sense that a person who believes in God is more religious than one who does not. However, this would require that we consider the person who says, "I'll believe anything they say just as long as I don't rot in hell" more religious than, say, a concerned theologian who completes a lifetime of concentrated and devoted study by humbly concluding that who or what God is cannot be known with certainty. We'd probably decide that this was a misclassification.

Without attempting to exhaust all the possible indicators of religiosity, I hope it's clear that we would never find a single measure that will satisfy us as tapping the real essence of religiosity. In recognition of this, social researchers generally use a combination of indicators to create a *composite measure*—an index or a scale—of variables such as religiosity. Such a measure might include all of the indicators discussed so far: church attendance, prayer, and beliefs.

While composite measures are usually a good idea, they do not really solve the dilemma I've laid out. With a little thought, we could certainly imagine circumstances in which a "truly" religious person nonetheless didn't attend church, pray, or believe, and we could likewise imagine a nonreligious person who did all of those things. In either event, we would have demonstrated the imperfection of the composite measure.

Recognition of this often leads people to conclude that variables like religiosity are simply beyond empirical measurement. This conclusion is true and false and even worse.

The conclusion is false in that we can make any measurement we want. For example, we can ask people if they attend church regularly and call that a measure of religiosity just as easily as Yankee Doodle called the feather in his hat macaroni. In our case, moreover, most people would say that what we've measured is by no means irrelevant to religiosity.

The conclusion is true in that no empirical measurement—single or composite—will satisfy all of us as having captured the essence of religiousness. Since that can never happen, we can never satisfactorily measure religiosity.

The situation is worse than either of these comments suggests in that the reason we can't measure religiosity is that it doesn't exist! Religiosity isn't real. Neither is prejudice, love, alienation, or any of those other variables. Let's see why.

There's a very old puzzle I'm sure you're familiar with: when a tree falls in the forest, does it make a sound if no one is there to hear it? High school and college students have struggled with that one for centuries. There's no doubt that the unobserved falling tree will still crash through the branches of its neighbors, snap its own limbs into pieces, and slam against the ground. But would it make a sound?

If you've given this any thought before, you've probably come to the conclusion that the puzzle rests on the ambiguity of the word *sound*. Where does sound occur? In this example, does it occur in the falling tree, in the air, or in the ear of the beholder? We can be reasonably certain that the falling tree generates turbulent waves in the air; if those waves in the air strike your ear, you will experience something we call *hearing*. We say you've heard a sound. But do the waves in the air per se qualify as sound?

The answer to this central question is necessarily arbitrary. We can have it be whichever way we want. The truth is that (1) a tree fell; (2) it created waves in the air; and (3) if the waves reached someone's ear, they would cause an experience for that person. Humans created the idea of *sound* in the context of that whole process. Whenever waves in the air cause an experience by way of our ears, we use the term *sound* to identify that experience. We're usually not too precise about where the sound happens: in the tree, in the air, or in our ears.

Our imprecise use of the term *sound* produces the apparent dilemma. So what's the truth? What's really the case? Does it make a sound or not? The truth is that (1) if a tree fell; (2) if it created waves in the air; and (3) if the waves reached someone's ear, they would cause an experience for that person. That's it. That's the final and ultimate truth of the matter.

I've belabored this point, because it sets the stage for understanding a critical issue in social research—one that often confuses students. To move in the direction of that issue, let's shift from sound to sight for a moment. Here's a new puzzle for you: are the tree's leaves green if no one is there to see them? Take a minute to think about that, and then continue reading.

Here's how I'd answer the question. The tree's leaves have a certain physical and chemical composition that affects the reflection of light rays off of them; specifically, they only reflect the green portion of the light spectrum. When rays from that portion of the light spectrum hit our eyes, they create an experience we call the color green.

"But are the leaves green if no one sees them?" you may ask. The answer to that is whatever we want it to be, since we haven't specified where the color green exists: in the physical/chemical composition of the leaf, in the light rays reflected from the leaf, or in our eyes.

While we are free to specify what we mean by the color green in this sense, nothing we do can change the ultimate truth, the ultimate reality of the matter. The truth is that (1) the leaves have a certain physical and chemical composition; (2) they reflect only a portion of the light spectrum; and (3) that portion of the light spectrum causes an experience if it hits our eyes. That's the ultimate truth of the universe in this matter.

By the same token, the truth about religiosity is that (1) some people go to church more than others; (2) some pray more than others; (3) some believe more than others; and so forth. This is observably the case.

At some point, our ancestors noticed that the things we're discussing were not completely independent of one another. People who went to church seemed to pray more, on the whole, than people who didn't go to church. Moreover, those who went to church and prayed seemed to believe more of the church's teachings than did those who neither went to church nor prayed.

The observation of relationships such as these led them to conclude literally that "there is more here than meets the eye." The term *religiosity* was created to represent the *concept* that all the concrete observables seemed to have in common. People gradually came to believe that the concepts were real and the "indicators" only pale reflections.

We can never find a "true" measure of religiosity, prejudice, alienation, love, compassion, or any other such concepts, since none of them exists except in our minds. Concepts are figments of our imaginations. Notice I did not say they are "only" figments of our imagination. I do not mean to suggest that concepts are useless or should be dispensed with. Life as we know it depends on the creation and use of concepts, and science would be impossible without them. Still, we should recognize that they are fictitious; then we can trade them in for more useful ones whenever appropriate.

Earlier, we looked at composite measures as a way of capturing a concept such as religiosity. This can be very useful, as I've suggested, but it can lead us down the wrong path. Sometimes we are better served by *disaggregating* concepts. Some medical researchers will say we will never discover a cure for cancer, but we might find a cure for breast cancer, a cure for prostate cancer, a cure for pancreatic cancer, and so forth. Similarly, it is useful to distinguish prejudice in terms of its target: racial minorities, African Americans, Asians, women, gays, Jews, etc. And for some purposes, it is best to disaggregate the dimensions of religiosity, even though they may be empirically correlated.

I have no intention in these comments of promoting or justifying research anarchy. You can't really get away with sticking a feather in your hat and calling it macaroni. As mentioned in Chapter 1, how we measure things is largely a function of agreement among the scientists working in a particular field of interest.

The creation of agreements regarding concepts is part of something more general, which I've discussed in Chapter 6, "Making Distinctions."

6

Making Distinctions

In this essay, I address an issue that is seldom mentioned in the context of social research, though it lies near the heart of what we do. I suggest that one of our primary tasks is to make distinctions within an undifferentiated field. Let me begin to explain what I mean.

As you look up from reading this book, you are confronted by a richly varied collection of things. You might take a moment to stop reading and look around you. While I can't know exactly what you have before you now, I can make up an illustration that probably isn't too far off the mark. To begin, there's this book, and the hands that are holding it. You may see a desk, a wall, perhaps other books. Maybe you can see some other people. That's what I mean by the things that confront you.

You implicitly assume, just as I do, that those things are all separate from one another. For example, your hands are separate from this book. Even if the book is resting on a desk, you assume that the book and the desk are two separate things. We say that such things are distinct from each other. In this discussion, I look at how things become distinct from each other and how they become distinguished from the whole they add up to.

Newborn babies seem not to make the distinctions you and I take for granted. As near as we can learn, newborns open their eyes and ears to confront a chaotic whole that William James, the founder of psychology, called "a blooming, buzzing confusion." Similarly, Jean Piaget, the renowned child psychologist, concluded that "in the [child's] first weeks of life the universe is not really cut up into objects, that is, into things conceived as permanent, substantial, external to the self and firm in existence . . ." (1954:5). As nearly as we can tell, newborn babies do not distinguish their hands from the rattle those hands hold and do not distinguish the rattle or the hands from the ceiling, the crib, or the bird perched in a tree outside the window. All those things are, for the newborn, unseparated regions of the whole patchwork quilt that confronts them.

While it would be easy to conclude (as we implicitly do) that you and I see things as they are and that newborn babies do not, I would urge you to withhold judgment on that matter for the time being. In the spirit of Chapter 1, keep it an open question.

Try looking up from this book and simply gazing at the scene that lies in front of you. Let your eyes go slightly out of focus; let things get a little hazy. Don't focus your attention on any one object. If you are successful in doing this, the scene before you will begin to resemble an unbroken patchwork quilt. If you happen to be gazing at a bookcase, for example, you will cease to see individual books. Gradually, they begin to bleed into one another, as if they were a slightly out-of-focus photograph of a bookcase and not the real thing. You lose your sense of three-dimensionality; things you normally regard as relatively near or far away now appear to be side by side.

It is interesting in this context that people who were blind at birth and who then gain their sight in adulthood (by an operation, typically) often report first seeing patches of color rather than the discrete objects that normal-sighted people see. For example, they would see a bookcase pretty much as I described it. This tends to confirm that the distinctions we make in the dividing up of our physical reality are acquired rather than natural or innate.

If physical matter is merely a complex arrangement of electrons, protons, and other subatomic particles, human beings obviously add a good deal to it. There is nowhere in physical reality a beautiful sunset, a stormy sea, a glistening rock, a mighty tree, or the color blue: all represent experiences we have somehow added to the colorless, odorless, endless, mindless flux and flow of minuscule particles. The universe, as we know it, is our own creation.

Even if the universe is just a flux and flow of particles, you and I do create patterns in it. We make distinctions within the unbroken patchwork quilt. We separate the land from the sea, the heavens from the earth, and the apples from the oranges. We do such a good job of our distinction making, in fact, that the distinctions seem real. Much of the way we create our experience of reality is socially grounded. I know you have read about the Eskimos having different words for numerous kinds of snow and about tropical tribes whose members distinguish many kinds of parrots. Such people see differences you and I cannot. By the same token, in some preliterate tribes the people can't see images in photographs; they can only see black-and-white or colored dots. All this should be enough to make you question whether seeing is really a sufficient basis for believing.

Many of the distinctions we make are linked to the social statuses we occupy. Look at the illustration below and identify what you see.

If you said "a tree," you get a small prize. Now, what else do you see? I suggest that your response will be conditioned by your past experiences and your present statuses. Some possible answers include:

- *Carpenter:* A few board feet of lumber
- *Poet:* "Only God can make a tree"
- *Ecologist:* Part of an ecosystem
- *Graphic designer:* Crummy drawing of a tree
- *Starving person:* Source of fruit or nuts
- *Little kid:* Possible tree house
- *Surveyor:* Landmark
- *Hiker:* Shade from noonday sun

Our differences don't much distinguish us from the bird who sees a homestead or the dog who sees a toilet. We are likely to see the tree very differently, depending on our social statuses. Moreover, our idiosyncratic past experiences may make us feel romantic, sentimental, angry, or lazy about the tree. The point is, it's just a tree (not to mention a flow and flux of subatomic particles); we add the other stuff on our own.

Now look at another illustration.

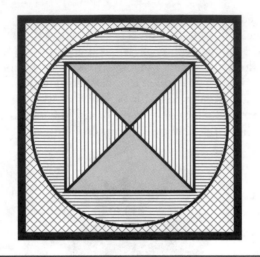

Figure 6.1

Which of the following do you see in Figure 6.1?

- Three squares
- Eight triangles
- A circle
- An occult symbol
- A computer graphics doodle
- All of the above
- None of the above
- Other

Any answer you give is correct, because what you see is what you see. But, what's really there? Is a circle really there? Are squares really there? How about rectangles? (Remember, all squares are also rectangles.) Do you see any polygons? (A polygon is a figure bounded by straight lines, which means that polygons include squares and rectangles; in fact, you could think of a circle as a polygon with an infinite number of infinitesimally small sides.)

Do you see the design as a teaching device? Do you see it as a problematic design element to be dealt with in the production of a book? Do you see it as a break in the monotony of words on the page? Was it a use of ink for you? (Perhaps a waste of ink?) Did you happen to say, "geometric design," or "symbol of our technological culture"? All those answers are correct—and also false!

The design is actually a flux and flow of particles. We humans added all the rest.

Now let's suppose you and I meet at the campus cafeteria. I'm sitting at a table, and you ask if you can join me. We introduce ourselves and begin to chat. Suppose it turns out that I'm a professor and you're a student. Take a moment to imagine how you might feel when you got that information. Then give a one-line summary of what has just taken place.

Whatever you said as a summary of what happened, see if you can also see the episode as:

- An instance of social interaction

- An example of status differences

- A description of cultural eating patterns

- A conversation

- The use of language

- An anecdote to share with friends

- The informal aspects of education

- An important learning experience

- A frightening experience

- An example of class-based oppression

- The beginning of a student rebellion

- The idea for a TV situation comedy

Once again we might ask: what was really going on in the story? Was it really any of the interpretations listed—or all of them? Actually, it was the flux and flow of particles. You and I added all the rest.

The process that separates the flux and flow of particles from the more interesting stuff we've considered is usefully seen as the making of distinctions. We distinguish one thing from another in the pulsing, undistinguished whole. Thus, we distinguish student from professor, oppression from empowerment, humor from tragedy, eating pizza from playing tennis, and so forth.

None of the distinctions you and I make are intrinsically right or wrong. There is no intrinsic difference between a ball and a strike, safe and out, fair and foul; we made all those up so we could play baseball. The difference between an A and an F is made up so we could play school. We made up the distinction between classical, jazz and rock so we'd be able to organize our music collection.

Filing is a clear case of distinction making. Suppose you've been given the task of filing case records in a social-work office. How should they be filed? Alphabetically? By case worker? By region of the city? By problem involved? Each of these possibilities implies a particular distinction, which all the others ignore. One of the important impacts of computers in such situations is that they allow the storage of records like these in such a way that they can be easily restructured and retrieved on the basis of many different distinctions. Thus, with a single computer command, you could pull out all the records involving the medical problems of people residing in the north end of town.

Making distinctions is clearly a fundamental human undertaking. It's also a central concern for science. Unfortunately, it is so basic an activity that we often lose sight of what's entailed. For the most part, the distinctions we make take the form of concepts. Sometimes, we begin with vague mental imagery and proceed to refine and specify it so that we can communicate about it to others with some clarity. At other times, distinctions are generated in a logical, deductive process.

Here are some examples. As a part of the ongoing attempt to achieve gender equality, people have noted that women have suffered from a structure of stereotypes, prejudice, and discrimination somewhat similar to the structures ethnic and racial minorities have experienced. As an aid to communication, the term *sexism* was chosen to serve the same purpose that *racism* has served in the racial context. People can now talk about sexism, discussing what does and does not qualify for that label and looking for ways to eliminate the conditions and practices the term represents. Some people prefer the more limited term, *male chauvinism*, meaning specifically male prejudice against women, but that term operates in fundamentally the same fashion.

Sometimes, our new distinctions arise as logical possibilities. Having made the distinctions of racism and sexism, we may reasonably look at other groups who experience similar structures of stereotypes, prejudice, and discrimination. *Ageism* is an example. By the same token, the distinction identified by the term *human rights* lends itself to the creation of *animal rights* and *rights of the unborn*.

It is important to note that the distinctions we make seem to be preceded by that which they represent. The conditions and practices we now call *sexism* or *male chauvinism* existed long before those terms were invented. It would seem to make sense, therefore, to say that we have simply invented words to stand for something that already existed. Don't accept that view too quickly, however.

It can be argued just as validly that sexism did not exist prior to the invention and communication of the term. Women weren't allowed to vote, to be sure. And women took their husbands' names—as well as their orders. Women were precluded from certain jobs and earned less money when they did the same jobs as men. All those individual things were true, but in an important sense they did not exist as a coherent whole until someone created the distinction and gave it a name.

To take a more bland example, did a royal flush exist before someone invented the game of poker? For as long as modern playing cards have existed, it has been possible to put together the ace, king, queen, jack, and ten of a particular suit. I suggest that the royal flush did not exist, however, until someone made that distinction in the course of inventing poker. In the same manner, someone created the distinction of a straight to include any numerical series of five cards (for example, a five, a six, a seven, an eight, and a nine) regardless of suit and the distinction of straight flush for straights of a single suit.

Public opinion didn't exist until someone created a distinction based on what the people think and gave it a name. Indeed, public opinion never exists about a particular issue at a particular time until someone sets about to discover what it is—then it comes into existence (and the person doing the looking cannot be separated from what comes into existence). This is discussed further in Chapter 8.

Many of the most important breakthroughs in social science involve the creation of new distinctions, such as:

- Social class
- Class consciousness
- Alienation
- Authoritarianism
- True believer
- Status inconsistency
- Social system
- Socialization
- Deviance

While it could be said that the "ingredients" of such concepts existed prior to the distinctions being drawn, the impact of drawing the distinctions per se is unquestionable. Thus, although it could be said that members of a particular segment of society constituted a social class prior to Karl Marx, his discussions gave the concept the reality it has for us today. Similarly, it could be said that members of a social class had always shared certain worldviews about their social status, but Marx's distinction of *class consciousness* gave it the reality it has had since that time. Nor can there be any question as to the practical, day-to-day impact those distinctions have around the world today.

Prior to 1897, it was generally assumed that the cause of suicide lay strictly in the domain of individual deviance. Every person who committed suicide had his or her own peculiar reasons for doing so, even though there might be classes of reasons, such as poverty, shame, or a failed love affair. In 1897, however, Émile Durkheim, the great French sociologist, published his classic *Suicide*, in which he reported broad-based societal causes for individuals' deciding to take their own lives. Durkheim found, for example, that some historical periods in particular societies were marked by a general sense of meaninglessness.

In times of war, revolution, or plague, for example, people's implicit assumptions about the meaning of life could be seen to break down. Old systems of right and wrong were challenged; people could no longer be sure of what was expected of them. Durkheim coined the term *anomie* in reference to such a societal condition, and his research suggested that conditions of anomie resulted in increased suicide rates. Although individuals still had personal, even idiosyncratic reasons for taking their own lives, the distinction Durkheim created opened the possibility that the act of suicide was not purely a result of personal choice.

Durkheim's research also indicated that certain subgroups within a society seemed differentially susceptible to anomie. Catholics, for example, seemed more immune than Protestants. In part, Catholics' strong sense of social solidarity seemed to give them a sense of meaning even in troubled times.

Since the publication of *Suicide*, social scientists have given a lot of attention to the impact of anomie. In 1956, Leo Srole, an American social scientist, drew another distinction relevant to the issue. He argued that the term *anomie* should be used only in reference to the kind of social condition Durkheim had discussed and coined the term *anomia* in reference to individuals' experiences of meaninglessness. Thus, Srole distinguished a social from an individual phenomenon. Srole then went a step further to develop a method for measuring anomia. The resulting Srole Anomia Scale has become perhaps the most frequently used scale in the social sciences.

Whereas Durkheim's distinction opened the possibility that the intimately personal act of suicide had social causes, Srole's distinction enabled scientists to understand that possibility more precisely. Research could now be undertaken to explain why, in a general social climate of meaninglessness, some individuals were affected by it and others were not.

As you can see, making distinctions is powerful stuff. Things may become real only through distinction making; at the very least, new distinctions focus attention on what was previously ignored, establishing importance and impact that did not exist before.

Powerful distinction making also creates problems. To the extent that distinctions seem to represent something preexisting and real, they generate what philosopher Alfred North Whitehead referred to as the "fallacy of misplaced concreteness." Most simply put, we come to take as real that which is not. Another term for this is *reification*. To reify is to treat an abstraction as physically real.

Reification is a common element throughout the patterns of distinctions we make in our social life. We make the distinction of *voter* in part by specifying that a person must be at least 18 years of age. Thus, the one day separating an 18-year-old from someone 17 years and 364 days old becomes far more significant than other days. Does that single day really make a person significantly more mature or responsible? Of course not. Only the distinction gives it its power.

The same can be said about drinking age, which varies from state to state. A single day changes the purchase and consumption of alcohol from a crime to permissible behavior. The differences from state to state highlight the arbitrary quality of the distinction, but the results are very real nonetheless.

All national boundaries are merely distinctions people have made in the past. Clearly, somewhat different boundaries could have been drawn without making much difference. Yet once territorial distinctions have been made, the one separating the French and the Germans, for example, or the one separating Iranians and Iraqis, they can become a matter of life and death. Other social distinctions such as those separating Protestants from Catholics,

Israelis from Palestinians, and bosses from workers become equally potent in practice.

This is not to say we should not make distinctions. As we have seen, distinctions can be valuable. Moreover, our most fundamental experience of reality is based on the distinctions we make and, importantly, on the distinctions we share with one another. The danger lies in our reification of those distinctions—in the pretense that they represent something preexistent and concrete.

Reification poses the same problem for science. Once scientists have agreed on the utility of a particular distinction, that agreement can present an obstacle to further inquiry and understanding. As a pointed example, consider the notion of objectivity in science, as discussed in Chapter 2.

Unarguably, the notion of objectivity has been valuable in the history of science. As a distinction, objectivity has helped free scientific inquiry from much of the impact of researchers' personal values and attitudes on the results of their studies. The commitment to objectivity, for example, makes it possible for Protestant researchers and Catholic researchers to conduct independent studies and reach the same conclusions regarding, say, the divorce rates and social class standings of the two religious groups.

By the same token, however, our commitment to objectivity poses a barrier to our grappling with philosophical issues such as those discussed in this chapter. By reifying the distinction, *objectivity*, we make it difficult at best for ourselves to entertain the possibility that objectivity cannot exist in social research—specifically, that the observer cannot avoid having an impact on what is observed. Thus, objectivity has largely become a closed answer rather than an open question.

The state of affairs I've just described explains why scientific progress is better described as a series of often radical, discontinuous jumps than as a smooth and continuous movement forward. It also explains why science is fascinating rather than humdrum and predictable.

PART 3

MODES OF
OBSERVATION

7

---ⓢⓢⓢ---

Quantitative or Qualitative?

One of the most basic divisions within the broad field of social research is the one separating *quantitative* from *qualitative* research. Essentially, quantitative research involves numerical analysis, whereas qualitative does not. The U.S. Census is a good example of quantitative research. So are public opinion polls. Historical studies and participant observation, on the other hand, are primarily qualitative, as is most anthropological research.

Most active researchers can be identified—and may identify themselves—as basically quantitative or qualitative in orientation. Likewise, some data-collection methods (such as surveys and experiments) are primarily quantitative, whereas others (such as field research) are primarily qualitative.

Often the division between quantitative and qualitative research in social science exhibits the same characteristics as other divisions in society: Hindus versus Sikhs, Russians versus Americans, blacks versus whites. Researchers with a quantitative bent sometimes look down on qualitative research as imprecise and unscientific; qualitative researchers sometimes regard quantitative research as superficial and sterile. My purpose in this essay is to consider the distinction between quantitative and qualitative research from a different perspective—one that allows us to scrutinize the nature of the distinction and to examine the relative strengths and weaknesses of the two orientations.

At the outset, most if not all data that social scientists collect are qualitative (non-numerical) at the outset. In the U.S. Census, for example, the census interviewer asks if your housing unit has an indoor toilet, and you say yes, or you put a check mark in a box beside that answer. In either case, the original datum just collected is non-numerical. *Quantification* occurs later, when your responses are transferred in the form of numbers (for example, "yes" = 1; "no" = 0) to computer files. A quantitative analysis occurs when Census Bureau researchers calculate the number of indoor toilets in America or the percentage of American households that have them.

Quantification, then, can be seen as a transformation of data from non-numerical to numerical form. This process is similar to the digitization of sounds in the production of digital recordings. Or consider the digitization of television images of Jupiter: a string of numbers sent back to the earth from *Voyager* and translated back into images on this end.

Alternatively, you might think of quantification as a grid superimposed over data that are themselves qualitative. This view is analogous to translating geographical locations into map coordinates. Thus, South Cape, Hawaii, the southernmost point in the United States, can also be expressed as 18°56'N latitude, 155°41'W longitude; and the easternmost point, West Quoddy Head, Maine, can also be expressed as 44°49'N latitude, 66°57'W longitude. South Cape is still South Cape, and West Quoddy Head is still West Quoddy Head, but it can be useful to superimpose the grid of map coordinates over these real (that is, qualitative) places—especially if you want to know the southernmost and easternmost spots in the nation. If you want to take a trip to the easternmost part of the United States, however, don't look for a bus marked 44°49'N latitude, 66°57'W longitude. If you want to send a letter, however, you should probably mention 04652 from the zip code grid.

To recap, data are fundamentally qualitative. Social researchers have an option of dealing with those data in their original, qualitative form or going a step further to quantify them. Neither approach is intrinsically better than the other. In fact, both have produced valuable results, from the beginnings of social research.

Max Weber's classic studies of the world's great religions offer evidence of the power of a qualitative approach. By immersing himself in the histories and sacred texts of Hinduism, Judaism, and Confucianism, Weber was able to identify important patterns in the relationship between religion and secular society around the world. By the same token, his historical examination of the beginnings of Protestantism demonstrated the critical role that religion played in the creation of capitalism. In that context, Weber introduced the German term, *verstehen*, or "interpretive understanding," to describe his analytical approach.

Émile Durkheim offers another illustration of the power of qualitative research in the domain of religion. His classic study of the Australian aborigines was based on his review of ethnographic reports from anthropologists who had observed the aborigines firsthand. At the same time, Durkheim's study of suicide shows the power of quantitative methods. By carefully examining the varying suicide rates reported in official government statistics of the regions and countries of Europe, Durkheim was able to develop sophisticated insights into the social causes of what otherwise seemed a very personal act.

George Herbert Mead was able to discern the role of social forces in developing the individual's mind and sense of self, without any numerical calculations to guide him. On the other hand, Samuel Stouffer's quantitative surveys of American soldiers during World War II revealed things about the way we judge our standing among our peers that were not otherwise evident. Clearly, both orientations have contributed importantly to what is known about human social life.

Although both quantitative and qualitative research are alive and well in social science today, it is also true that quantitative research enjoys a higher status in certain ways. Over the past few decades, quantitative research has typically been viewed as the wave of the future in various social science disciplines. It has commonly been associated with the younger generations of scholars. New faculty members with new PhDs often arrive on campus with quantitative skills, language, and appetites that may puzzle and even threaten their older colleagues. Universities have invested millions of dollars in equipment and facilities to support quantitative research. University departments of government have been renamed departments of political science. The transformation of departments of speech into departments of communication represents another facet of the shift to quantitative orientations. Even where names have not changed, interests have. Not too many years ago, geography meant the listing of national imports and exports; today, it includes complex equations explaining migration patterns.

What accounts for the generally higher status of quantitative over qualitative research? There are undoubtedly a great many reasons. In part, quantitative social science profits from the general homage Americans give to science. The mystique of the computer compounds that factor. In fact, I suggest that the computer is to social science what the microscope was to biology and what the telescope was to astronomy.

When computers started becoming commonplace on university campuses in the early 1960s, they were not especially appropriate for work in social research, being tailored primarily to the physical sciences. Whereas the physical sciences commonly required a great many complex calculations to be performed on relatively small sets of data, social science required rather simple calculations to be performed on large data sets. Since more research money was available for research in the physical sciences than in social science, computers and their programs not unreasonably gravitated toward the physical sciences. By the end of the 1960s, however, powerful programs for social research began appearing, and social scientists became more active and ambitious.

The arrival of the microcomputer in the late 1970s posed a new dilemma for social scientists. The small, affordable machines, first desktops and then laptops, were easily powerful enough to undertake many of the most commonly used analyses, but they could not manage the large data sets. Subsequent years, however, have seen remarkable advances in the data storage capacity of computers, and we have witnessed what is sure to become a golden age for quantitative social research.

In addition to the fairly simple processing of large data sets, current computers will support statistically complex operations, such as factor analysis, smallest space analysis, and computer simulations. One social scientist sitting at a desk will now be able to undertake analyses that would have been beyond the means of a team of researchers and a large campus computer thirty years ago. The computer, then, has brought special advantages to quantitative, as opposed to qualitative, research. However, the potential uses of computers in qualitative research are considerable as well. Here are a few examples.

One of the least exciting parts of field research in the past has been the reproduction, filing, and cross-referencing of notes. Typically, the researcher spends time observing whatever is under study and taking notes if possible. Later, the notes are used in preparing a more fully detailed account of the events; and once the expanded field notes have been composed, copies are made so that any particular entry can be filed in several different categories of interest.

Suppose you are observing a campus political demonstration. The students are upset at the firing of a popular professor and have been sitting in front of the administration building for a week. You've been observing the demonstration every day, taking notes on what happens. On the seventh day, the fired professor gives a speech to the crowd, thanking the demonstrators for their support and urging them to stay true to their principles. Reviewing your notes later on, you might like to store a copy of your detailed notes on that speech in a special file for "nonstudent participants" and another copy in a file dealing with examples of "solidarity maintenance," as well as keeping a copy in your chronological file of all events. Physically, this took the form of cut-up sheets of paper stuffed in file folders.

In the past, this process required a good deal of photocopying, clipping, and highlighting. But today, the detailed notes can be stored digitally rather than on paper. If you still want to create the equivalent of file folders, you can easily mark portions of your notes and transfer them electronically to the appropriate files. However, it may be more effective to maintain one master file and insert code words (such as "solidarity maintenance") where appropriate through your notes. Your word-processing system can then be instructed to search for all the places where the code appears. Or, of course, you can search for anything else—names, places, and so forth.

This is only one example of how computers can powerfully assist qualitative research. Laptop computers or tablets can be taken with you to the scene of the action, so that you can either make notes directly—if that's appropriate to what you are observing—or duck around the corner and record your notes there, while the events are fresh in your mind.

Later, when you are writing a report on your research, you will be able to extract quotations, information, or portions of your interpretations and move them electronically into the report. This saves time and keystrokes and also avoids mistakes that can creep in whenever you retype something.

You can do all this using the basic applications that came with your computer. However, there are now a number of powerful programs available for qualitative social research. NVivo, ATLAS.ti, Qualrus, and many others are now available to support data collection and analysis by qualitative social researchers.

While this use of computers in qualitative social research may seem to pale in comparison with the calculation of regressions, factor analyses, and simulations derived from masses of quantitative data, don't think it's not as powerful an application. The advent of the computer allowed quantitative social researchers to undertake extensive analyses that had been possible (with much more labor) even before the computer; similarly, the computer with a word-processing system allows a qualitative social researcher to undertake more extensive and intensive analyses than were feasible in the past.

Realize that I've only discussed one quite specific use of the computer in qualitative social research. There are many other uses, access to digital library files, for example. The computer is thus not exclusively a boon to quantitative researchers, although some people seem to feel that computers and qualitative research somehow are inherently incompatible. (In stark contrast, some people now feel the computer has enabled them, at last, to write poetry, which they could never quite do with pen and paper.)

Serious social researchers should keep both quantitative and qualitative options open in addressing any research question. To do otherwise would be similar to an artist who only uses green paint—a severely limiting repertoire. The primary strengths of quantitative methods are:

- *Specificity:* measurements and other design aspects are typically more explicit, so we know exactly how the research was carried out and what decisions were made.

- *Replicability:* because of the specificity, an independent researcher can more easily repeat the study and see whether the same conclusions are reached.

- *Generalizability:* if proper samples have been selected, the results of the research can be taken to reflect the state of affairs in the larger population.

In contrast, qualitative research typically involves more judgment calls by the researcher. The (quantitative) survey researcher may define *liberal* as anyone who answered "liberal" to the question, "Are you a liberal or a conservative?"; the (qualitative) field researcher, on the other hand, may listen to everything the person has to say on a variety of issues and make a summary decision as to how the person should be categorized. The problem with the latter method is that we may not know exactly how or why the researcher made such decisions. It follows, then, that an independent researcher would be hard-pressed to replicate the research. Moreover, we cannot be sure how accurately qualitative research conclusions reflect the whole population. The primary strengths of qualitative research are:

- *Flexibility:* a qualitative approach permits the researcher to adapt quickly to changing conditions and/or new insights.

• *Degree of depth:* by not having to use a standardized inquiry in all observations, the researcher can probe more deeply below the surface.

• *Gestalt:* where the quantitative researcher must pinpoint and focus, the qualitative researcher can be open to all aspects of the situation—facial expressions, sounds, weather, smells, and so forth.

In measurement quality, qualitative research tends to be stronger in matters of *validity*, and quantitative research tends to be stronger in matters of *reliability*. Thus, in the example used above, the qualitative researcher who listens to all a person has to say and then renders a judgment of "liberal" or "conservative" would seem to have made a "truer" measure of political orientations than the survey researcher who asked, "Are you a liberal or a conservative?" The latter seems a superficial measurement, and even when several questionnaire items are used in the construction of an index or scale, the fundamental standardization in quantitative research seems to detract from the validity of the measurements made.

On the other hand, the quantitative measures are clearly more reliable, in that they would be likely to produce consistent results if the measures were made repeatedly and by different researchers. We have less confidence that the qualitative measures would remain consistent in such a situation. We might change our minds and decide the person is more conservative than we thought, or we might disagree about how particular views ought to be categorized.

Quantitative and qualitative research methods not only have different strengths and weaknesses, they also complement each other perfectly. I realize that I run no risk in urging social researchers to use both quantitative and qualitative methods. That's about as controversial as saying we should tell the truth and be decent to each other. And yet the fact remains that researchers face a powerful tendency to tilt one way or the other.

There is some justification for specializing in this respect, of course. All research methods require training and experience, so it's not unreasonable that we might each want to become good at something rather than being mediocre at everything. Science and society presumably benefit from that desire. But the dangers in such specialization are considerable.

Quantitative researchers can become so enamored of statistical artifacts as to mistake them for what they can only partially represent or reflect. If you've ever found yourself being dealt with as though you were your IQ, grade-point average, or SAT score, you've had a practical experience with this tendency.

Researchers inclined only to qualitative methods run the risk of mistaking opinions for observations and feelings for findings. Numbers are a useful device for keeping ourselves honest. (Interestingly, socialist countries have sometimes introduced profit mechanisms as a device for independently measuring efficiency and effectiveness.)

All of us employ both quantitative and qualitative methods in the rest of our lives. We accept that highway speeds are measured in miles per hour; we also recognize that you can't adequately quantify the cuteness of baby goats or the beauty of a sunset. At the same time, the apparent conflict between the quantitative and the qualitative is present in all aspects of our lives. Priests and ministers know that the size of a person's offering is not an adequate measure of his or her religious devotion, but it's not altogether irrelevant either. We distinguish between how much money a person has and how the person got it. We know that height doesn't make you a good basketball player, but no one hires five-foot centers. In short, the dilemma inherent in whether to approach research quantitatively or qualitatively is mirrored in life generally. Perhaps life imitates science instead of art.

8

---❦---

The Impact of the Observer

During the late 1920s and early 1930s, a team of social researchers in the Chicago area undertook a series of industrial research studies that were to become more famous for their methodological flaws than for anything substantive they discovered. F. J. Roethlisberger and W. J. Dickson were interested in learning what might be done to improve worker productivity in the telephone bank-wiring room of Western Electric's Hawthorne plant. On the whole, it was a fairly common research proposition.

Imagine you were a worker in the Hawthorne plant's bank-wiring room at the time the study was conducted. All day long you sat at a workbench, soldering wires to telephone switching panels. As the researchers were to discover, the workers had developed informal quotas for productivity, so you would have learned how many units you were expected to produce in a day, and you would have developed your own work routines to keep you in line with your co-workers' expectations.

Then one day, the team of researchers arrived. Carrying clipboards and forms, they wandered about in the workroom, observing you and your co-workers, making notes, and talking quietly among themselves. It would have been no secret that the researchers' purpose was to find ways for increasing productivity, and you would have been a little uneasy about how their findings would reflect on your image as a worker and on your future employment. So you would have continued working, watching the researchers, alert to the implications of their studies.

Finding the bank-wiring room rather dimly lit, the researchers decided that increasing the level of lighting might improve productivity. They brightened up the workroom—and to their delight, productivity increased. Following the timeless principle that "anything worth doing is worth doing to excess," the researchers then increased the lighting further, and productivity increased again. In fact, every time the researchers came into the bank-wiring room and increased the lighting, the workers' productivity improved!

Had the researchers quit with their discovery that increased lighting improved productivity, we might never have learned of their study. But now they did something that might seem a little perverse to a nonresearcher: they went back into the bank-wiring room and dimmed the lights. To everyone's amazement, productivity increased again!

The previous increases in productivity, it seems, were not so much a function of better lighting as of the research process itself. The workers in the bank-wiring room knew they were under special scrutiny, since they had been singled out by the researchers. And whenever the researchers made a change in the lighting, the workers came under more scrutiny. Unconsciously, perhaps, they all worked a little harder.

I have often thought of forming a management consulting firm, which I would call "Hawthorne Research, Inc." The firm would promise to increase worker productivity for clients and would make good on the promise merely by focusing attention on the workers. There would be no need to draw clever conclusions from the research; simply doing it would increase productivity.

This suggestion should not be regarded as heartless or anti-worker, by the way. Conducting research that focuses attention on particular procedures in any organized social endeavor causes those involved to be more conscious about what they are doing—and often leads them to see new possibilities that were not previously evident. Consider a company that gets a little of its new business through incidental referrals from satisfied clients, without making any special effort to encourage referrals. Just conducting research to discover how many new clients are produced in that fashion almost inevitably leads to increased referrals. Workers who may never have thought about suggesting to clients that they refer others to the firm begin to make such suggestions once they know the research is underway.

From a strictly scientific perspective, the studies at the Hawthorne plant dramatized the need for social scientists to be wary of the impact of their research on the subjects they were studying. In fact, social scientists have coined the term *Hawthorne effect* in reference to the impact of the observer on the observed.

There are many other examples of the impact of the observer in social research. Just prior to World War II, Hadley Cantril, a survey research pioneer, wanted to find out how Americans felt about the likelihood of the United States getting into the war. Realizing that people's opinions might be influenced by the way the question was asked, Cantril conducted two large, comparable national surveys. The two surveys were designed in such a way that each should have given an accurate measure of the attitudes of the American population regarding the likelihood of our entry into World War II. Had he asked the same question in both surveys, Cantril should have gotten virtually identical results in each—but he asked different questions.

In one survey, Cantril asked, "Do you think the U.S. will succeed in staying out of the war?" Two-thirds said they thought we would. In the other survey, Cantril asked, "Do you think we'll eventually get involved in the war?" Two-thirds said they thought we would. Clearly, the wording of the questions had a powerful impact on the answers.

All social scientists are aware of this issue in social research, and it is usually an easy one for students to appreciate. It's my feeling, however, that we generally treat the issue in a rather perfunctory manner—not recognizing the extent of its significance for research and for life.

Over the years, social scientists have developed numerous ways of dealing with the possible impact of the observer. Questionnaire designers have attempted to write neutral questions that will not influence answers in one way or another. Interviewers are trained to be neutral in asking questions and in their responses to the answers they receive.

The classical experimental design, with its control groups, is another method for dealing with the impact of the study on what's being studied. This can be seen most easily in a medical example. Suppose we've developed a new treatment for the common cold. If we simply give the treatment to a bunch of sufferers to test the treatment's effectiveness, we can't be sure of why they get better. They may get better even if the new treatment doesn't really do anything, as sometimes happens when medical researchers administer hocus-pocus treatments—like sugar pills (placebos). Like the Hawthorne plant workers, they respond to the attention they are receiving and perhaps to the belief that they are receiving some powerful medicine. *Control groups* are one way to guard against situations like those described above. In the medical example, we might select two groups of sufferers, give one group the new treatment, and give the other group some make-believe treatment. If our new treatment is really effective, it should do better than the fake. But although social scientists have developed a number of techniques to guard against the impact of the observer on the observed, the problem runs far deeper than such techniques would imply.

Sometimes, when I tell the Hadley Cantril story about attitudes toward our entry into World War II, students ask, "Which was the right way to ask the question? What *was* the American attitude about getting into the war?" The answer is always less than satisfying.

There was no correct way of asking the question, and there was no true answer. Ultimately, there was no overall American attitude about the likelihood of our getting into the war.

To be sure, individuals had attitudes on the matter—attitudes that existed within the context of how each individual saw things. Since I was one year old at the time of Cantril's surveys, I can assure you that I had no opinion in the matter, but if I had been older my attitude probably would have shifted somewhat from day to day, depending on events in the war zones, statements by public officials, and changes in my overall pessimism or optimism on a given day. Probably the same was true for most other Americans.

If this is difficult to grasp, take a minute to look at your own attitude toward the likelihood of, say, the United States getting into a war with Russia. Since we can't look into the future to know for sure what will happen, all we have are our opinions—supported, perhaps, by more or less information and careful thought. If you are anything like me, your attitude shifts back and forth over time.

Moreover, I'll bet that your attitudes on this are susceptible to influence by other people. You've probably had conversations that left you feeling pretty pessimistic about our prospects for the future, and you've probably had other conversations that left you more optimistic. If that's happened to you, you're fairly normal. The alternative is to have your opinions rigidly locked in place, immune to any external influences. You probably don't have a single, fixed opinion about the likelihood of the United States and Russia going to war. What you may *say* your opinion is depends a lot on how you happen to be feeling at the time someone asks you for your opinion.

In a sense, then, you didn't have any opinion about the likelihood of war until I raised the issue a moment ago. Unless you already happened to have been thinking about the possibility of war when I mentioned it, you didn't really have an opinion at that moment. You had the makings of an opinion: you had memories of times when you discussed the matter or thought about it in the past (including the opinions you formed at those times); you had memories of the opinions others have expressed in conversations and in books and articles you've read; you had the way you happened to be feeling in general as you were reading the book. In short, you had what it takes to form an opinion, so when I brought up the example and asked whether you thought a war was likely, you may have been able to state an opinion (or not, as the case may be). But, you didn't actually have an opinion during the instant prior to my raising the question.

If you think about it, what I've just described is probably true almost any time people are asked a question on a survey. When Hadley Cantril's respondents were asked for their opinions about the likelihood of the United States entering the war, they probably didn't have an opinion at the instant they were asked. So, they had to make up opinions, using whatever resources they had on hand. The opinions they made up were influenced by their memories of past discussions and past decisions, by what they had heard others say, by how they were feeling at the time of the survey, and by the wording of the question.

What we've been examining on an individual basis is even more telling for the social whole. Clearly, the American people as a whole did not have an opinion as to the likelihood of the United States entering the war, though individual Americans were able to create opinions when asked in a survey.

The point of this discussion is that the observer and the observed may be inextricably linked. While we should certainly employ all the techniques available for ruling out observer effects as much as possible, it is impossible to eliminate such effects altogether. If that sounds like bad news, it may also—somewhat perversely, perhaps—be good news. While we can regard irreducible observer effects as a methodological failing, we can also regard them as a key to understanding the fundamental nature of human social life.

We can learn something from physicists in this regard. The Hawthorne effect has a counterpart in physics called the Heisenberg uncertainty principle. In 1927, Werner Heisenberg demonstrated that it is impossible to measure both the location and the velocity of subatomic particles simultaneously because measuring one affects the other. Moreover, this situation is not merely the result of imperfect measurement techniques; it is inherent in the natures of location and velocity themselves.

Since Heisenberg's contribution of the uncertainty principle, researchers in subatomic physics have increasingly attempted to include the observer in their understanding of the observed. In contrast, social scientists have attempted to avoid observer effects rather than acknowledging them and including them in our understanding of how life operates. This is ironic because the impact of the observer in social research is much more obvious— at a commonsense level—than it is in subatomic physics, and yet physicists have adopted a more sophisticated approach to the matter than have social scientists. In fact, some physicists have begun talking about the role of consciousness in shaping the nature of physical reality, so that they often sound strangely like Eastern mystics.

Everything I've been saying about the impact of researchers is true about the impact of everyone else in a society. My suggestion that your opinion about the likelihood of war was actually created in response to my question applies with equal force whenever someone else asks you how you feel about U.S.–Russian relations. The opinion you express, therefore, might be more appropriately regarded as the product of a social interaction than as an expression of a preexisting viewpoint. Notice how this approach begins to call for a radically different paradigm of social reality.

What I was originally calling "the impact of the observer" might actually be an essential source of reality rather than something that can distort it. Put simply, you just might not even have opinions until you have occasion to express them in social interactions.

In these most recent comments, I have purposely neglected to include things you read or things you see on television or on the Internet. Although they have a definite impact on your knowledge and on the opinions you express, they differ importantly from human interactions. Seeing something on TV or reading something online does not necessarily result in your expressing an opinion. When you are called upon later to express an opinion, you may use the materials you saw or read, but the opinion itself still may not exist until it is expressed.

I become increasingly convinced that a great deal of social reality is a function of communication. Obviously, promises and similar commitments can't exist unless they are communicated.

And while we speak of making promises to ourselves, my experience has been that such promises have far more power when they are communicated to others. (For example, tell your spouse that you've promised yourself you'll work out at the gym every day, and the likelihood that you'll honor the promise is much greater than if you keep it your own little secret.) By the same token, requests don't exist unless communicated. If you would like to have an extension on the deadline for your term paper but don't mention it to your instructor, what you have is a hope or a prayer, not a request.

We could extend the list of obvious examples of things that don't exist until and unless they are communicated, but I am suggesting something far more fundamental. Much or even most of what we think resides in our heads may not actually exist until we communicate it. Let's look again at your opinion as to the likelihood of a war with Russia.

I ask you if you think there'll be a war, and you either say that you do or that you don't (or that you don't know). Once you've put the opinion into words, we can say that it exists. It has form (words) and location (in your mouth and in my ears). But did it exist prior to that time? If it did, what was its form? Where was it located? Although something seems to have existed prior to your expressing your opinion, it's not at all clear what it was or where it existed.

If your opinion didn't exist until the moment it was expressed through communication, then the opinion itself is inseparable from the social context within which it was created. The "impact of the observer" doesn't interfere with our knowing what your opinion is; the observer is actually a co-creator of the opinion.

What does all this mean for social research? Does it mean there is no point in conducting surveys and asking for people's opinions, for example? Not at all. If what I've suggested is true, then the co-creation of opinions applies to routine social life as much as to occasions of social research. By influencing the attitudes we measure, we are tapping into a normal social process.

The chief methodological implication is that we should always be explicit about the way in which our data were collected and should demand that other researchers be equally explicit. Whereas we might previously have been satisfied with an assurance that a researcher's design was such as to minimize any impact of the research process itself, that approach is not appropriate within the paradigm I've been describing.

Here is a practical example of the implications of this para-digm. Sometimes, you encounter research reports—usually in the mass media—that announce findings about, say, liberals and con-servatives. Often, such reports fail to describe exactly how people were assigned to those political categories, or they may include a vague reference to the use of scores from a "scale of political atti-tudes." We usually regard such reports with a certain amount of annoyance at their lack of methodological detail, but we may then go on to assume that the researchers made their measurements more or less appropriately.

The preceding discussion, however, implies that we can make no such assumption, since there is no generally appropriate way to make such measurements. The assignment of one person to the lib-eral category and another to the conservative is every bit as much a function of the questions asked as of the answers given. Without knowing the questions asked, we simply do not know what the terms *liberal* and *conservative* mean in the study at hand. By the same token, we can't know how to take any findings related to those labels—that whites are more conservative than blacks, for example.

This problem is most critical in simple descriptions. Consider this campus newspaper headline: "Conservatives Outnumber Lib-erals 3-to-1 at State University."

Because college students are typically expected to be more liberal than the general population, a research finding like this one would attract a lot of interest. Not only are conservatives in the majority, according to the report, they are in the overwhelm-ing majority.

In the actual situation I've taken this illustration from, the researcher had purportedly used a "standardized scale of political attitudes," though the name of the scale was not identified. Nor-mally, we would take some comfort in knowing that the researcher had used a measure previously used, and presumably refined, by other researchers. In this case, however, it was also reported (as an aside) that the researcher had changed the wording on a few of the scale items in an effort to make them more appropriate to the particular students being studied. To the casual reader, this would seem an appropriate step. But notice that standardization has now flown the coop. Finally, in the technical details of the report, it was noted that the scale-score cutting points for distinguishing liberals and conservatives yielded 5 percent liberals and 15 percent con-servatives—meaning that 80 percent of the students were not des-ignated as either liberal or conservative.

Usually when I recount this research example, students conclude that the research findings were worthless, and that's not a
bad conclusion to draw. However, the findings may be even less
than worthless: because we don't know how the measurements
were made—what questions were asked and how the answers
were treated—we don't have enough information to know
whether the findings are of any value.

My purpose in this essay has been to open up a new paradigm
with regard to scientific measurement. I haven't tried to present a
neat package, all tidy and complete. Rather, I hope to engage you
in an ongoing investigation.

Even apart from the philosophical aspects of the issue, the
reporting of measurement details in a research report is not
merely useful, it is vital. Moreover, such details are not merely
necessary for advanced scientists who may wish to study the
results in greater-than-usual depth; they are vital to anyone who
wants to draw any conclusions from the study's findings. A
researcher who fails to report the precise details of measurement
is akin to a sportscaster who reports all the football scores without identifying the teams involved.

9

The Power of Introspection

The normal process of social research very often involves assumptions and inferences about what is going on in the heads of the people we study. Why do some men oppose equal employment opportunities for women? In part, we think it involves fears about competition for jobs. Some may feel that their manhood is threatened when women perform jobs previously seen as "Men's Work."

We explore such hypotheses by asking men about their feelings in these regards. This is no easy matter, however. You might address the job-competition issue by asking about women "flooding the job market" or taking jobs from men with "families to support" or by using similar language that would seem to make opposition to equality more acceptable. But how are you going to ask men if they feel their manhood is being threatened? Admitting to feeling threatened would be the same as admitting defeat.

At times like these, it would be great to be able to look inside the heads of the people under study. It would certainly be useful if we could get inside some man's head and actually overhear him saying "My God, if my wife starts driving a semi, she's going to think I'm a wimp! What will my son think of me? I'll probably have to quit the bowling team." That kind of inside view would certainly be useful as we set about trying to understand why people behave the ways they do. Well, in this chapter, we're going to look at the most convenient and least expensive research technique available to the social researcher, although it is seldom talked about. I refer to your ability to learn about human beings by observing yourself—from the inside.

There's a bit of irony involved in using introspection as a method of studying human beings. On the one hand, beginning students in the social sciences often start out with the problem of thinking all human beings are just like them and like the people they grew up with, or at the very least that people are supposed to be like that. We sometimes use the term *ethnocentrism* to describe this tendency, and one task of any introductory course in the social sciences is to bring students to an acceptance of *cultural relativity* instead: recognition that there are many different cultural patterns and practices in the world, and that none is inherently superior to the others.

Therein lies the dilemma. While we recognize ourselves to be human beings—like the people we study—we generally regard ourselves as vessels of truth rather than as fit subjects for detached observation and analysis. My purpose in this chapter is to open up the possibility that you can study yourself as an effective way of learning about humans. Here's an illustration.

For much of my adult life, I have been concerned with the problem of overpopulation, which I see as the "mother of all social problems." When I first began hearing about this problem at the end of the 1960s, there were about 3.6 billion people on the planet. Today there are twice that many! Crowding aside, there are countless problems that flow from overpopulation. Here are just a few.

With a fixed amount of food produced, an increase in mouths to feed means less for each mouth. However, other needs of an expanding population—for example, housing, highways, schools, hospitals—require land that might have been used to grow food. Experts disagree on precisely how long the remaining fossil fuel reserves will last, but no one argues that they are infinite. On the other end of human consumption, the pollution we create increases as there are more of us polluting. And where some societies are fortunate enough to enjoy rising standards of living, their citizens produce even more pollution than previously.

While there are disagreements about how many people could live on this planet, I don't think anyone would disagree that there is *some* limit. Angsley Coale, a famous demographer, once calculated that if human world population were to continue growing at the current rate, by the year 3000 the mass of human bodies would be expanding out from earth faster than the speed of light.

Okay, there's a starting point. Since Einstein told us that nothing can travel faster than the speed of light, we are safe in assuming it won't ever be quite that bad. In fact, long before we realized Coale's calculation for the year 3000, we would be piled on top of each other enough to crush the people on the bottom. And long before that, we would be jammed together so tightly we wouldn't be able to reproduce—or want to try. And well before that, we would have drunk all the water and eaten everything is sight. In sum, the question is not whether population growth will stop but when and at what level—and on whose terms? Mother Earth's solutions are not too pleasant, so we might want to handle the problem ourselves on nicer terms.

The cause of this population growth is pretty simple to understand; there are more births than deaths each year. The solution is equally simple: since no one wants to solve the problem by increasing death rates, we need to reduce the number of births. People need to have fewer babies on the average. If every woman had two children, she would replace herself and her mate, and overall population would remain stable. (Since some children never have children themselves—e.g., die before having children—the replacement number is slightly higher than 2.0.) If only all our problems had such simple solutions. Right? So why don't people simply apply that solution?

It is perhaps ironic that I began learning about this problem at about the same time I was being blessed with my first child, Aaron. Since I was newly initiated into the process of producing children, I had a front-row seat for studying opposition to the need for fewer babies. You see, the first time I began hearing about the problem of overpopulation, I didn't want to face it. The more I learned, however, I reached a point where I felt countries like India and China had too many people. Still later, I was willing to agree that "large welfare families" would be better off with fewer children.

Finally, I experienced an overpopulation epiphany. Driving home from the university one day, I found myself sitting in the middle of an ever-more-common traffic jam on the freeway. I began looking into the cars parked around me, and I was struck by the realization that they were not filled with Indians and Chinese. I didn't even see the stereotypical large welfare family. Actually, I saw people just like me (and typically one per car). I realized in that moment that the overpopulation problem I was experiencing was caused by people like me. Shortly after this freeway revelation, I got a vasectomy and made a tiny contribution to the reduction of population growth.

Overpopulation has continued to concern me, and my initial resistance and denial have given me an opportunity to observe some of the factors that may cause resistance in others. One of the first issues was that of personal freedom. I didn't want the government, the UN, or Zero Population Growth telling *me* how many children I could have. This was eventually resolved when I recognized that I had never wanted to have a big family. I was an only child and loved it, just as my son reports for himself. (At one point he wanted a big sister, but I explained the difficulty of achieving that.) As I have become an activist in the fight against overpopulation, I have found my initial concern for my freedom was not unique to me. Others sometimes talk in those terms. The first time I appeared on a panel to debate the problem of overpopulation, I found myself opposed by someone from the ACLU, an organization I had belonged to for years. The 'L' in ACLU, as you no doubt know, stands for Liberty.

Then I noticed I was wondering what my parents and extended family would think about my failure to people future family reunions and insure the preservation of our family name. (I was adopted, but no matter.) I recall my mother once telling me she had always been taught that "you take care of your children when they're young, and they take care of you when you're old." My fiercely independent Vermonter mother added, "That ends with me." The more I have studied the issue of population, I've found not all Americans have my mother's independent streak, and in many poorer societies children are referred to as a form of "social security," the only protection for those too old and infirm to care for themselves.

From a broader perspective, I had some concerns for what a sudden reversal of the pattern of population growth would do to the economy and other aspects of society. Diaper and baby food companies would take a hit, and so would obstetricians and pediatricians. Then the dominos would fall on elementary school teachers and up through the grades. As a college professor and textbook author, I realized I would not be exempt from the effects of a declining birth rate.

While I noticed I was willing to pay the probable price, I recognized that my financial benefit from continual growth was not as great as it would be for others. *Vested interest* became a critical element in understanding and remedying overpopulation, as well as other social problems. It is not difficult to understand why the petroleum industry, for example, resists the development of solar power and all talk of climate change. There are gigabucks at stake.

It is obvious to me that what I see inside my head is not altogether unique. While I can't pretend to know what you may have seen if you also did the exercise of looking at your own thoughts and actions regarding overpopulation, we almost certainly have some similarities and overlaps. Looking honestly into your own mind thus can give you some insights into what is going on in other people's heads. It won't tell you for sure, but it can suggest some fruitful possibilities. Introspection is a useful form of *exploratory* research. The insights you gain through introspection can then be tested by other means. In the case of overpopulation, I've used insights gained introspectively to inform my discussions with others. Sometimes it seems clear to me that another person is operating from the same internal principles as I saw in myself; at other times this doesn't seem to be the case. Since I am still very much in the midst of this inquiry, I don't have any definitive results to offer, but I am clear about the value I've gained from the introspective explorations—which I continue.

Following are a few more illustrations for you to practice introspective inquiry on.

Stereotypes and prejudice. If you look at yourself honestly, you will probably find that you have a great many more stereotypes and prejudices in your head than you would like people to know about. I've noticed, for example, that I still have stereotypes about women in positions of leadership: either that they can't handle the job at all or that they have to give up their femininity in the process. In case you wondered what happened to the stereotype about beautiful blondes being stupid, it's alive and well in my head. Whenever I see a beautiful blonde woman, I'm likely to have that thought. When a woman tells me she's an active feminist, I have the thought that she hates men, that she may be gay, and that she has no sense of humor.

You can imagine how embarrassing such thoughts are for me, and you can bet I don't talk about them a lot. I only bring them out now to support you in developing your introspective abilities, and I suspect your own stereotypes and prejudices would be fruitful ground for you to explore. Take a moment to look at some of the stereotypes you have regarding men and women, racial and ethnic minorities, and other kinds of people who may come to mind.

In my more conventional research on prejudice, it had never occurred to me that I still retained the kinds of opinions described above and simply acquired additional opinions that contradicted them. Though I knew I once had the opinion that beautiful blondes were stupid, I discovered through introspection that I still have that one and have added to it the personal observation, "No, they're not." Moreover, I found that I've trained myself to behave in accord with, "No, they're not."

Discovering you have prejudices and stereotypes you thought you'd given up can be disappointing, but it's also an opportunity for learning more about how humans operate. Stereotypes and prejudices are a part of your life's experiences; it's not really surprising that they persist like other memories and habits. Furthermore, I've discovered that those thoughts need not have any impact on how I feel and act. Now when I notice myself having the thought that a beautiful blonde is probably stupid, it's truly a "passing thought." Usually I find it humorously quaint, like an old-time advertisement. It also seems to me that those thoughts come by less frequently than they did when I jumped in to beat them off with their opposites.

Political ideologies. Take a moment to review your political point of view. What do you believe in and stand for? Against the backdrop of that general review, consider each of these political issues and state your position.

• Abortion

• Women's equality with men

• Same-sex marriage

• Climate change

• Welfare

• Capital punishment

• Tax-supported national health care

I suggest that your specific political views are largely a function of what's expected of someone with your general outlook, and those views are enforced by others who share your general outlook. Thus, if you're a liberal, you pretty much have to support the welfare system, even if you actually think it's made matters worse rather than better. Or if you're a conservative, you may feel irresistible pressure to deny the idea of climate change, even if you recognize the scientific consensus that it's real.

Even if these specific examples don't apply to you, some honest introspection can show you instances of positions you do feel obliged to support, even though you don't really believe in them.

Discoveries like that can reveal aspects of political ideology that you may not have seen before.

Morality. Morality lives close to ideology. Introspection can shed light on your own views of what constitutes moral behavior, as well as offering insights into morality in general. It is useful to begin by separating positions that are deeply and fundamentally true for you from those based primarily on what others will think of you. Here are two specific examples from my own experience that may help guide your own inquiry.

Late one night, many years ago, I was taking a babysitter home after she had sat with our son for the evening. Arriving at her house, I waited in the car with my headlights lighting her way as she went up the driveway, through a gate, and across a patio to the door to her house. Although I couldn't see her very well once she went through the gate, I caught a glimpse of her hand waving over the wall, and then the outside light by the door was turned off. As I pulled out of the babysitter's driveway and headed home, I had the thought that I had been very responsible in waiting until she was safely inside her house before I left.

Then I began fantasizing about various ways in which my precautions might not have been enough. Suppose there had been a mugger waiting just inside the house; the babysitter's waving hand might have been a result of her struggle to escape. The mugger might have turned off the light to conceal what was happening. These sorts of fantasies, I suppose, are not unusual in our TV action-thriller culture. What I saw as the fantasies unfolded was unsettling, however.

With our babysitter now in the clutches of a sex-crazed killer, you might expect that I would be looking at ways I could have been more responsible in the matter. Should I have walked her to the door? Should I have instructed her to flash the lights three times as a signal that everything was all right? But I wasn't having any of these thoughts. Instead, I imagined myself talking to the police and to her parents, telling them the precautions I had taken, and they were all agreeing that I had done everything anyone could expect.

At that point, I recognized the extent to which I substitute public opinion for real results. While I would have been upset at our babysitter's getting mugged, I was more concerned that no one should think it had been my fault. That's not exactly good news to get as a human being, but it's a useful insight for a social scientist.

Here's a similar example. Driving home from the university one day, I had a front-row seat for watching a young woman in a sports car swerve across the highway directly in front of me to avoid hitting a car in the lane to my left. Realizing she was going off the road to the right, she overcorrected and was soon headed directly across the highway toward the left. Trying once more to correct, she hit the center divide and her car flipped end-over-end along the left-most lane of the freeway, eventually coming to a stop upside down.

The car to my left came to an abrupt stop a few feet from the overturned vehicle. I drove past and cut into the left lane just beyond it. Jumping out of my car, I arrived at the wreck at the same time as the driver who had stopped just short of it. The sports car was upside down, resting on the door tops and hood, having crushed the windshield. Glass was everywhere on the highway, a liquid we first thought was gasoline but which turned out to be engine coolant was spreading a dark shadow outward from the car. And there was a limp arm sticking out from under the overturned car.

The other driver and I threw ourselves at the car, attempting to roll it over and rescue the young woman pinned underneath. I remember that I grabbed the rear wheel and lifted and pushed with all my strength; the other guy did the same at the front of the car.

We failed. Although we were able to lift the car part way, we weren't able to roll it all the way over. The car settled back in its upside-down position.

Now here's the point of the story. What went through my head was that I had given it the old college try. Embarrassed as I am to say it, I can recall looking at my hands and seeing how black and dirty they were from grabbing and lifting the tire; I knew I could show those hands to other people, and they would say, "You did your best." To tell the truth, I was ready to wait for the police or the fire department to arrive.

My partner, the other driver, reacted differently. While I stood there looking at my hands, he had run a few steps toward the grow- ing line of stopped cars and uttered a few magical incantations my publisher will not let me put in this book. Suddenly, people came pouring out of those other cars, and within seconds half a dozen of us were easily rolling the car over and extricating the victim.

As in the case of the babysitter fantasy, my willingness to look honestly at my own thoughts revealed aspects of responsibility that were not as vividly clear before. You can undoubtedly learn something of value by looking at your own thoughts in that regard. This chapter may have left you with a dilemma. My main message is that you can learn about humanity by carefully examining yourself, but you should not imagine that everyone is like you: two seemingly contradictory ideas. This situation calls for a high "tolerance for ambiguity." This refers to the ability to hold seemingly contradictory ideas in your mind without the need to choose between them.

Consider the question of responsibility for how things turn out for individuals in a society, which we discussed in Chapter 4. Is poverty, let's say, the responsibility of the poor individuals or the responsibility of the society? There are arguments to be made for both views and some evidence can be found to support each. A poor person who takes the position that he or she can rise above such social constraints will benefit from that point of view. From the standpoint of a compassionate society, however, it is appropriate to look for the social causes of poverty—those things beyond the control of the individuals suffering from it. Laying the responsibility on society is disempowering for an individual, even though evidence can be marshaled to support the view that society is responsible. Holding these two ideas may call for a degree of tolerance for ambiguity.

The tolerance for ambiguity is generally regarded as a sign of intellectual maturity. But consider this: science can be seen as a war against ambiguity. Scientists want to make sense out of things. Contradictions are anathema to scientists. Scientists are intellectuals, aren't they? So is the tolerance for ambiguity a good thing or a bad thing? There's another marvelous opportunity for you to exercise your tolerance for ambiguity. Take it out for a spin. See what it can do.

In summary, introspection is a fertile opportunity for insights into the operation of human society. There are two key points to bear in mind. First, you must be honest with yourself, realizing that it may not be comfortable to do so. You don't have to tell anyone what you see, however; in fact, you don't have to justify it to yourself. Be detached, as though you were watching someone else's slide show. Second, never forget that introspection is exploratory, not definitive. Don't assume that everyone thinks the way you do, but use the insights of introspection as a jumping-off point for more rigorous testing.

PART 4

ANALYSIS
OF DATA

10

Finding Patterns

If you take a moment to gaze casually around you, it's possible to experience all you see as chaotic and unorganized. For example, I find myself looking at a desk computer, an iPhone, an iPad, a stapler, a roll of masking tape, a coffee cup, and so forth. My desk isn't particularly messy, but still there's no apparent pattern to the way items are spread out on it.

You can also see the course of your life that way. Even if you are on what seems a pretty rigid schedule, the specific events of your day have a random quality. You're reading a book; the phone rings; a friend wants to get together for lunch next week; you begin brewing a pot of coffee; the cat cries to be let out; you open the door and find a package from the delivery service; and so forth. Life seems to unfold in unexpected ways.

Finally, the flow of social life around you seems to have this same random quality. Again, you can see what I mean by looking around you or by remembering the last time you were in the presence of several people. Perhaps you're walking down the street. Up ahead of you, you see a young man mailing a letter to his sweetheart as a bakery truck passes by on its way to a supermarket where the manager is approving a check being cashed by a young divorcee who has a new account since her former husband ran away with the waitress who had only taken a job in the diner because her mother needed an operation to remedy the hearing problem she developed when her next-door neighbor's boiler exploded one night because the husband's nephew had tried to fix it after the sewers backed up. . . . Life is a lot like a soap opera.

Given the explosion of apparently random yet interconnected events all around you, your task as a social researcher is to find coherent patterns. Social research proceeds on the premise that social life is not completely random, but that it behaves in accordance with certain laws or principles—that the seeming chaos can be seen to make sense.

Examine the geometric design presented in Figure 10.1, and try to find the pattern in it. I can assure you that the design does have a genuine regularity to it; your job is to find it.

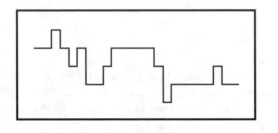

Figure 10.1

If you weren't able to find a pattern in the drawing, don't feel bad. It's impossible to see. Still, I didn't lie to you as regards its regularity. The drawing is the sum of three very regular patterns, shown in Figure 10.2.

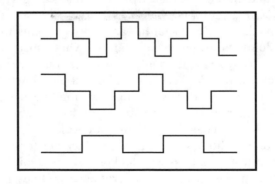

Figure 10.2

If you study the three regular patterns for a bit, you'll see how the original drawing is the sum of these three. The erratic quality of the first drawing is due to the different cycles of the three patterns that produced it.

This effect has real-life correlations. Georg von Bekesy, a physiologist who earned the Nobel Prize in 1961 for his work on the functioning of the inner ear, once told me of an example from his native Hungary.

It seems there was a large lake in Hungary that was a popular resort. For centuries, Hungarians had flocked to the lake for vacation during the summertime. One year, the water level in the lake was unusually low. The next year, it was even lower. And the year after that, it was lower still. Those who owned vacation homes on the lake were in a panic. There were rumors that a hole had opened at the bottom of the lake and that the water was slowly draining out. Homes were sold at a great sacrifice, as people anticipated the lake's drying up to nothing.

Dr. von Bekesy and two of his colleagues decided to look into the matter. The government had been maintaining official records of the water level of the lake for several hundred years, and the young researchers were able to confirm that this was the lowest the water level had ever fallen.

Next, they began looking for cyclical natural forces that might affect the water level. I can no longer remember the actual factors, but there were three of them, and they were something like the phases of the moon—except that they varied more slowly. Each of the factors the researchers looked at was likely to affect the water level in the lake, and each had its own cycle that pressed for a high water level sometimes and a low water level at other times, on a regular schedule. Moreover, the researchers found that the recent years in question represented the first time in recorded history that all three factors simultaneously pushed for a low water level.

By seeing the lake's water level as the product of three separate factors, each with its separate cycle, von Bekesy and his colleagues were able to explain past fluctuations and—the good news—to predict that the water level would begin rising again in the years to follow. Sure enough, the lake's water level began rising year after year, just as von Bekesy and his colleagues had predicted.

The aim of social research is to discover regular patterns in social behavior. Some of those patterns are descriptive and some are explanatory. As an example of descriptive regularities, consider the morning rush hour on a freeway near you. Between 7:15 and 8:50, perhaps, traffic is bumper-to-bumper. Then it lightens up. At around 10:30, you can drive anywhere you want with no delays. What's especially interesting is that this pattern is much the same day after day, five days a week, even though the individuals involved may differ. One person may go to work early one day and later than usual the next day. Another person may stay home from work altogether one day, and a tourist driving cross-country may happen to arrive just as the rush hour is beginning. Despite these idiosyncrasies, the rush-hour traffic looks the same day after day. In other words, a pattern is present in the whole that is not dependent on regularities at the level of the individuals involved. Still, many of the people involved in rush hour are operating pretty regularly as individuals; but consider the following example.

In 2007, the registered birth rate in the United States was 14.3 per 1,000. In other words, for every 1,000 Americans alive at the beginning of the year, on average 14.3 babies were born over the course of the year. The total amounted to over 4 million babies. Now, imagine the circumstances involved in the birth of some of those babies. In one case, a married couple that had delayed having a child until their careers were established finally succeeded in conceiving after three years of trying. In another case, an unmarried high-school girl got pregnant unintentionally; after discussing the situation with her boyfriend, she decided to have an abortion; when her parents heard what was happening, however, they persuaded her to have the baby, which they agreed to adopt. In another case, a working wife simply got fed up with her job, stopped taking the pill, and became pregnant. There was also the ambitious, corporate junior executive whose boss told him the company preferred to place its trust in family men; the young man who had been taught he wasn't really a man until he had produced a child; the young woman who had been told something similar about being a real woman; and the couple who needed to produce an heir or lose the pimple cream fortune. (Did I mention that life is like a soap opera?)

There were over 4 million stories like these across America in 2007. No two were exactly the same. Few of the 4 million new mothers talked to each other or even knew each other existed. None of the new parents needed a permit to produce babies. (You need a fishing license but not a baby-making license.) There were no state or federal quotas. Each couple acted independently. Over the course of the year, it all just sort of turned out the way it did— and that happened to total 14.3 births per 1,000 population.

In 2008, another set of soap operas unfolded. There was a woman who arranged to be artificially inseminated with the sperm of a Nobel laureate, because her husband, a prominent scientist in his own right, had always dreamed of sharing his love of science with a son or daughter but proved to be sterile as a consequence of some early experiments with radioactive isotopes while a graduate student at a major Midwestern university. Then there was the young man of rather modest ethics who persuaded his out-of-town date for the harvest ball that he had had a vasectomy, when in fact it was only a tonsillectomy; she chose to have the baby in the belief that her date would marry her, even though he had not given her his correct name or city of residence.

None of the 2008 stories was exactly the same as any other story, nor was any exactly the same as any in the 2007 crop. On the whole, 2008 was a replay of the chaos of 2007, except that the players were not the same. Although some of the 2008 crew were repeaters from 2007, most were not. But in 2008, the overall birth rate amounted to 14.3 per 1,000, identical to 2007. How could that be? Was it simply a coincidence? Let's look at some more birth rates for the United States (U.S. Census Bureau, 2012, p. 65):

Year	Birth Rate (per thousand)
2001	14.1
2002	13.9
2003	14.1
2004	14.1
2005	14.0
2006	14.3
2007	14.3
2008	14.3

Clearly, something is going on here that cannot be accounted for by central planning in the federal government or by people working together to achieve a common goal. Out of chaos and idiosyncrasy at the level of the individual, an amazing regularity is generated at the level of society. Even after more than forty years or so as a practicing social scientist, I find that simply astounding.

Birth rates, moreover, are not just a bizarre anomaly in an otherwise haphazard and chaotic society. The death rate in 2008 was 8.1 per 1,000. While many individuals were recorded officially as having died of the same cause (such as heart attack), we know that no two cases were exactly the same. Moreover, unlike the case of birth rates, we know there were no repeaters in later years. Now look at a few death rates over consecutive years (U.S. Census Bureau, 2012, p. 65):

Year	Death Rate (per thousand)
2001	8.5
2002	8.5
2003	8.4
2004	8.2
2005	8.3
2006	8.1
2007	8.0
2008	8.1

These birth and death rates are not biological regularities defining the way human beings are; they reflect social and cultural differences. Yemen's 2008 birth rate, for example, was 38.5; Japan's was 8.7. Moreover, these other nations' annual rates were, by and large, just as regular as the United States'. Witness Japan's and Yemen's birth rates, for example (see http://www.indexmundi.com/facts/indicators/SP.DYN.CBRT.IN/compare?country=eg#country=jp:ry).

	Birth Rate (per thousand)	
Year	Japan	Yemen
2001	9.3	40.4
2002	9.3	40.0
2003	9.2	39.6
2004	8.7	39.4
2005	8.4	39.1
2006	8.7	38.9
2007	8.6	38.7
2008	8.7	38.5

This is not the place to identify all the factors affecting birth rates at a societal level, but you can probably imagine what some of them are. The availability of birth control techniques has an obvious impact. Religion has an impact: Catholic countries have relatively high birth rates, for example. Economic factors make a powerful difference: poor countries have higher birth rates than rich ones. Different cultures have different modal opinions regarding the desirability of large or small families. The list goes on and on.

Birth and death rates are not the only regularities in society. A similar story could be told about many other social statistics—

divorces, dog licenses, the incidence of various diseases, auto accidents, the number of books returned late at public libraries. The
plain fact is that the members of a society are, *as a whole*, amaz-
ingly regular, even when they are unpredictable as individuals.

You may recall an earlier discussion of Durkheim's classic
study of suicide. Even though every suicide victim had a unique
story, Durkheim discovered consistent patterns in the suicide
rates of different regions and countries. Moreover, he was able to
suggest explanations for those patterns. Finding that predominantly Catholic regions and countries had lower suicide rates
than predominantly Protestant regions and countries, he suggested that Catholicism provided its followers with a stronger
sense of meaning in life. (We might add that the Catholic Church
also teaches that suicide is a sin.)

The social researcher's job, then, is to discover social regularities and to explain them. The regularities need not be constant
over time. Some patterns are steady increases, others are
decreases, and still others fluctuate up and down in a regular way.
In any case, neither the discovery nor the explanation of regularities is as routine as it may appear.

First, explanations for regular social patterns come and go.
Today's explanation of choice is tomorrow's naive misconception,
and it makes no sense to think we will ever discover the real
explanation for anything, particularly when discovering truth so
often changes it (as we saw in Chapter 1).

Lest you think this changing "truth" marks a shortcoming for
the social sciences, consider the ever-changing advice we receive
from the field of nutrition. Are eggs good for you or bad? How
about coffee or red wine? Actually, all sciences are open-ended,
scientists need to keep open minds, and our knowledge of the
world keeps changing as a consequence, as we saw in the Chapter
1 discussion of the "half-life of facts."

Similarly, while today's regular pattern may persist tomorrow, we may uncover an even more regular pattern that makes
more sense than the one we first saw. The birth and death rates
discussed above, for example, are *crude* rates (rates based on total
population size), whereas *age-specific* rates (rates within specific
age groups) may show different patterns. Moreover, age-specific
birth and death rates are more useful in understanding what is
happening within a population over time.

Between 1900 and 1940, for example, the death rate for Americans age 85 and older decreased from 260.9 per 1,000 to 235.7

per 1,000, a modest decrease of 10 percent. This represents advances in medicine and in public health, as well as other factors. During the same period, the death rate among Americans under one year of age declined from 162.4 per 1,000 to 29.6 per 1,000—an 82 percent drop! Clearly, greater strides were made in reducing infant deaths than in extending the lifespan of the elderly.

In explaining why regularities exist, the researcher operates in the deterministic world of cause and effect, as discussed in Chapter 4. Chapter 11 takes another look at causation.

11

---·⟨≾∽◉⟨◉∽⟩⟩·---

Probability and Causation

A news report some years ago focused on four New Mexico teenagers who had died of heart attacks in recent years. While it is unusual for teenagers to die of heart attacks, that wasn't the real reason for media interest. In every case, they suffered heart attacks because of highly excited nervous systems. Their nervous systems sped up so fast that they suffered cardiac arrest and died.

Perhaps this story still seems incomplete to you. Why did they develop such highly excited nervous systems? All four had been sniffing typewriter correction fluid. "Oh," you say. "Now I understand." Now you can see why the four deaths were deemed worthy of media attention.

But, do you know the full explanation for their deaths? For example, why were they sniffing typewriter correction fluid? A part of the answer should include the fact that other possible intoxicants—including alcohol and marijuana—were not legally available to teenagers. If these had been available, perhaps the four teenagers wouldn't have been sniffing typewriter correction fluid.

The picture is still incomplete. For the prohibition of alcohol and marijuana to have made any difference, the teenagers needed to have some desire to get high. Why did they want to get high? Poverty could have played a part, although I don't know what their socioeconomic statuses were. Maybe they were alienated from the mainstream of American society, or they had grown disillusioned with the state of the nation or of the world, or they had despaired that world peace would ever be achieved, or they had wanted to escape the superficial and hypocritical workaday world of modern American society.

Suppose any of these things was true for the teenagers in question. Would you be willing to see those factors as the cause of death? A young person who found no meaning in life sought to escape into intoxication, was prohibited from using alcohol or marijuana, turned to typewriter correction fluid because it was available and legal, suffered an excited nervous system that caused cardiac arrest, and died.

From the point of view examined in our discussion of determinism in Chapter 4, everything that had happened prior to a particular teenager's death was a contributing cause. Figure 11.1 illustrates part of a hypothetical causal web that could have accounted for the death of one of the New Mexico teenagers. The diagram includes only a tiny fraction of the causal factors we might consider in such an analysis. Even so, I think you'll see how complex the matter is.

Notice how the teenager's final cause of death in this illustration depended on each and every one of the factors shown. For example, if the community had had better medical facilities, the teenager's life might have been saved, despite all the other factors. Similarly, perhaps a different family resistance to heart attacks might have made the difference. Or at the other end of the diagram, a treaty to eradicate all nuclear arms might have taken away the teenager's desire to get high.

Causation is no simple matter, even though we talk about cause and effect every day in countless situations. We say you did poorly on a test because you didn't study. You had a traffic accident because your brakes needed adjustment. You snapped at your best friend because you stayed up too late and drank too much coffee. You didn't follow your true love into that weird religious cult because you're a Capricorn. We have causal explanations for just about everything in our lives.

As these examples illustrate, our causal explanations are usually far simpler than those in the diagram I just presented. For every "why" question I might pose, you are likely to offer one reason. Only my probing for more is likely to produce additional causes, and it's extremely unlikely that you will ever produce an explanation looking anything like the diagram.

Take a minute to consider why we treat matters of cause and effect in such an oversimplified manner. I'm less interested in what your answer to this question is than in how many answers you arrived at. Did you come up with a single answer to my question? I did, when I posed the question to myself. My answer was

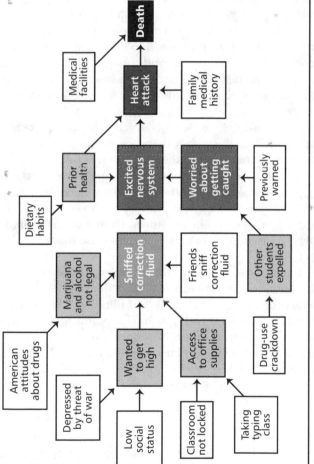

Figure 11.1   A Hypothetical Causal Web

that it wouldn't be feasible for us to give each other long lists of causes every time such questions arose, so we usually limit ourselves to the most important one. That was what I considered the most important cause of our tendency to oversimplify causation.

As I continued to think about the matter, I found other answers. For example, we usually look for causes in order to be able to affect the situation we are in—or to affect similar situations in the future. Once you know your accident was caused by faulty brakes, you know what to do to avoid future accidents. Thus, it seemed to me that we only want to know causes that can make a difference. That was my second answer. Had I pressed myself further in the matter, I'm sure I could have created a new diagram with numerous contributing causes for our tendency to oversimplify causation.

Whatever the reason(s) for our observed tendency, we seek simple explanations. And this is not merely a foible of non-scientists. In science, the goal of parsimony explicitly favors simple answers over complex ones. We might describe parsimony as getting the most understanding out of the fewest number of explanatory factors. That's part of the attractiveness of Einstein's famous $e = mc^2$: the energy that could be produced from a chunk of matter was simply the product of its mass (m) times the square of the speed of light (c).

In social science, as in the natural sciences, there is a premium on parsimonious explanations. What determines how a person will vote, for example? There are millions of answers, of course. But social research on voting behavior points to a few factors that are more potent than others. Economic status has a powerful influence on voting behavior, for example. Race and religion also influence voting. So does the voting history of the family the person grows up in: there's a good chance you'll vote the way your parents do.

The important difference between this voting-behavior illustration and the earlier diagram about the teenager who sniffed correction fluid and died is that the earlier diagram dealt with factors that (hypothetically) actually caused the person's death, whereas we are now looking at factors that may affect voting behavior. The two illustrations would be comparable if we were now discussing why you voted the way you did in the latest election, but let's shift to the issue of possibilities and probabilities.

Many factors may determine voting behavior, including those mentioned above. But what does it mean to say, "may determine"? It means that, in any given case, the factor in question may produce the effect, or it may not. Thus, in the next election you may vote the same as your parents, or you may not. That's not especially useful to know, however. It's obvious that you will or you won't. It would be a lot more useful to know how likely it is that you'll vote the same as your parents.

Some degree of likelihood exists in this sense. You may feel virtually certain that you will vote the same as your parents, you may think the likelihood is just about zero, or you may feel it's completely a toss-up. Regardless of what you feel the likelihood is, what makes you think any such "likelihood" even exists?

Probably your sense of this rests on your observations of the past. You may have noticed you've never voted the same as your parents so far, and you can't see any reasons for that to change now. Or you may have voted the same as your parents in every election since you could first vote. In either case, you implicitly assume that what you will do in the next election will generally follow the patterns of the past. Put slightly differently, you assume that how you vote in the next election is a specific instance of a larger phenomenon we might call "how you vote in general." We make assumptions about the specific instance based on what we've observed about the larger phenomenon.

Let's switch now from the word likelihood to the term probability, as it is used in science. Probabilities are expressed numerically in science. To take a simple example, if you roll a single die (half a pair of dice), what's the probability of getting a two? First, there are six possible rolls: one, two, three, four, five, and six. Of the six possibilities, only one is a two, so we say the probability of rolling a two is 1/6 or 0.1667. Every time we roll the die, that's the probability of getting a two.

Given that, what's the probability of getting a two if you roll the die six times? It's not 6/6 because you can't be certain you'll roll a two even if you roll six times. In fact, to elaborate on the example, the probability of rolling a one, a two, a three, a four, a five, and a six in those six rolls is extremely low.

There are actually two levels of probabilities in this example. First, the probability of rolling a two on any particular roll of the die is 1/6. This means that if you roll the die 600 times, about 100 of those rolls should result in twos. The second level of probability concerns the word about in the preceding sentence. There is a certain probability that you'll roll exactly 100 twos, another probability that you'll roll 99 or 101 twos, and so forth. Put together, these probabilities tell us what to expect and caution us not to be too sure.

Let's return to the voting example. Suppose you've cast 100 votes altogether during your voting career (counting several votes on any given ballot). Moreover, let's assume that you've compared notes with your parents and discovered that you and your mother, say, have voted the same ninety times and have voted differently ten times. What's the probability that you and your mother will vote the same in the next election?

Lacking any other information, our best prediction is that you will vote the same as your mother nine out of ten times on the new ballot. If there are twenty offices and measures to be voted on, we'll predict that you and your mother will vote the same on eighteen of them. As in the case of rolling the die 600 times, however, this doesn't mean you'll vote the same on exactly eighteen of the offices and measures, but we'd expect it to be close to that. If you disagreed with your mother on every vote, that would mark a radical departure from the pattern of the past.

The probabilities in the case of rolling the die are determined deductively—that is, we figured them out. Those relating to your voting habits were determined inductively—that is, based on the past patterns we've observed. There's no way we could calculate the probability of your voting like your mother the way we calculated the probability of rolling a two. We just assume that future voting will be more or less the same as past voting.

Now let's look at the way causation and probability operate in social research. To begin, probabilistic causation in social research is almost always inductively determined. That is to say, patterns observed in the past are used to reach conclusions about the way things are in general. Rather than observing a particular person for the purpose of understanding or predicting what that person will do in the future, we study a large number of people for the purpose of understanding and predicting what people in general will do.

In contrast to the example of your voting behavior, social research looks to the attitudes and behaviors of many individuals and attempts to uncover causal relationships that may apply to people in general. Social researchers are not actually interested in whether you vote the same as your mother, but we are interested in the extent to which people vote the same as their mothers in general. If that factor can account for a large portion of voting behavior, we are very much interested in knowing that.

By the same token, it is interesting to social researchers that people in the lower economic strata are more likely to vote for the Democratic Party than are those in the upper economic strata. As in our earlier discussions, causation is probabilistic here as well. Not all poor people vote Democratic, and not all wealthy people vote Republican. Nevertheless, there is something about economic status that has an impact on voting behavior in general. Causation is expressed as a matter of probabilities. Thus, we may say that 80 percent of the poor (defined in some fashion) vote Democratic in contrast to 35 percent of the rich.

The determination of causes, however, is as much a matter of creation as of discovery. Although we tend to operate as though there were causes to be discovered, the truth is that we create causal relationships through our analyses. We select from among the many causal factors that have impacts on the dependent variable. What we select today will be supplanted by the scientific creations of tomorrow. The lesson of Chapter 1 bears repeating in this context. Once we learn something about the operation of social life, that very knowledge may lead to a shift in how society operates.

Traditionally (in recent decades, at least), working-class Americans have voted Democratic. When there have been many working-class people, the Democratic Party has been successful in electing its candidates and enacting its social programs. Moreover, many Democratic social programs (such as minimum wage and unemployment insurance) have eased the plight of the working class. As a result, many who once turned to the Democratic Party for aid have improved their life situations to the point that the social programs associated with the Democrats are no longer relevant to them, and the Democratic Party has lost voters. Please realize I am not implying that voting is only or even mostly based on economic self-interest. Indeed, a common discussion in recent years has focused on the tendency of poor white voters to vote Republican, clearly basing their votes on values other than economic self-interest. (Wealthy Democrats, of course, are an example of the same phenomenon.)

These are only a few of the issues that help make the matter of causation a complex one in social research. I complete this discussion by offering a question for you to ponder. Consider for a moment some fairly straightforward examples of cause-and-effect relationships. For example, women support the Equal Rights Amendment more than men do, and no one would quarrel with the conclusion that gender is an important cause of those attitudes. Similarly, old people are more likely to oppose cuts in Social Security than young people are; again, age unquestionably causes attitudes in that respect, granting the probabilistic quality of that causation. Finally, during the 1950s and 1960s, black people supported the Civil Rights Movement more than white people did; and there is nothing puzzling about that difference either.

I suggest that each of these examples—along with hundreds more we could think of—are reasonably cut-and-dried illustrations of causation. Granting that sex, age, and race, respectively, were not the only causal factors involved, and that they did not determine people's attitudes 100 percent of the time, there is simply no question that they caused attitudes in the sense in which we've been using the term causation in this chapter. My question is, when did they cause those attitudes? When does causation happen?

12

Critical Thinking

Science is often described as *logical/empirical*. In this chapter, I look at the logical half of that pairing. In addition to agreeing with what we observe, scientific conclusions need to make sense. More accurately, the scientist must make sense out of things. Sense is not something that just happens. However, making sense is not quite as straightforward as it might seem.

Unfortunately, there are few cut-and-dried rules for making sense in connection with social research. The discussions to follow raise some of the issues involved and offer illustrations that will help you explore the question for yourself.

Let's begin by recalling that the logic of scientific research has both deductive and inductive aspects. *Deductive* logic is sometimes defined as reasoning from the general to the specific, while *inductive* logic proceeds in the other direction, from the specific to the general. The classic example of deductive logic is the syllogism:

All men are mortal.
Socrates is a man.
Therefore, Socrates is mortal.

Inductive logic, on the other hand, begins with concrete, empirical observations and seeks general patterns in them. For example, study after study indicates that American women earn less money than men, even when they perform the same work, have the same credentials, and so forth. The pattern of those findings suggests that a general principle is at work: women are discriminated against in the workplace.

Both deduction and induction are vital to critical thinking in science, and the two approaches complement each other.

Galileo was responsible for a major breakthrough in our understanding of gravity. I can recall a classroom demonstration that involved a long glass tank containing a stone and a feather. The tank was tipped up vertically so that both the stone and the feather were at the same end. Then the tank was quickly flipped upside down. Both the stone and the feather fell to the other end, but of course the stone fell much faster than the feather. Then all the air was pumped out of the tank, and afterward the stone and feather fell at the same speed. This demonstration supported Galileo's contention that gravity worked equally on all objects, but that air resistance slowed the feather more than it did the stone.

Galileo's view conflicted with the generally accepted Aristotelian position. Aristotle had said that objects that were alike in size, shape, smoothness, and other respects but that differed in weight would fall at speeds proportional to their relative weights. For example, a chicken egg that weighs one one-hundredth of what a marble egg of the same size weighs will, according to Aristotle, fall only one one-hundredth as far in the same period of time. In fact, this is demonstrably untrue, so it's somewhat surprising that Aristotle's view was accepted for so long.

But Galileo also argued that the Aristotelian position didn't stand up to deductive scrutiny. Galileo reasoned as follows. If different objects have different rates of free fall depending on their weights, then even different volumes of the same material will have different natural speeds of fall. Two stones of identical composition, one of which weighs twice as much as the other, should thus have free-fall speeds of, say, 2 and 1 units, respectively.

Now, what happens when the two stones are bound together and then dropped? On the one hand, the stone whose natural free-fall speed is 1 unit should retard the speed of the stone whose natural free-fall speed is 2 units; on the other hand, we now effectively have a single stone heavier (and therefore, by definition, faster) than the heavier (and faster) of the two original stones. Therefore, the effect of binding the two stones together is to make a package that simultaneously falls faster and falls slower than the heavier of the two original stones. In this manner, Galileo demonstrated deductively that Aristotle's position was false. Galileo thus created and substantiated a universal law of gravity through a combination of deductive and inductive reasoning.

While it's not possible to lay out an effective cookbook for making sense in science, the following format is often a useful one.

- Observe the way things are.
- Ask why they're that way.
- Suggest an explanation.
- Then ask, "If the explanation is correct, what else must also be true?"
- Look to see if it is true.

You use this line of reasoning in daily life already. Let's say you're a woman working for a large corporation. After a few years in the same position, you begin thinking that your supervisor is prejudiced against women in business, and that's why you haven't been promoted.

While people often stop at this point in their reasoning, we can easily go farther. If it is true that your supervisor is prejudiced against women in business, other women in the office are probably not being promoted either. Specifically, we should expect that women in the office are not being promoted as quickly as men—if your conclusion regarding prejudice is correct. Now, the next step is obvious: find out how long the average man and the average woman must wait for a promotion in your office. If men are promoted substantially faster, that observation would support your conclusion about prejudice. If men and women are, on average, promoted at about the same rate, then you may need to give up your explanation and look for another one. Once you have an explanation that agrees with empirical observations, essentially the same format can be used in challenging that explanation and in answering challenges from others. Thus, once you think you've found the correct answer: (1) ask what other explanation could account for the same observations; (2) ask what else should be true if the alternative explanation is correct; and then (3) check to see if the implications of the alternative explanation are borne out by additional empirical observations.

You'll recall that when Émile Durkheim studied the official suicide rates of different European countries, he found among other things that predominantly Protestant countries (like Germany) had higher suicide rates than did predominantly Catholic countries (like Italy). Durkheim offered the explanation that religion had an influence on suicide—specifically that Catholics were less likely to commit suicide than Protestants.

Given the difference between Germany and Italy, however, we could certainly think up other explanations that had nothing to do

with religion. Italy was south of Germany, for example. Perhaps suicides were affected by climatic conditions rather than by religion.
Maybe people didn't commit suicide as often in warm climates.

If this alternative explanation were correct, Durkheim reasoned, then suicide rates should be lower in southern Italy than in
northern Italy, lower in southern Germany than in northern Germany, and so forth. His empirical observations, however, did not
consistently support the alternative.

Durkheim brought the same critical attention to bear on his
own conclusions. If religion really had an impact on suicide, then
predominantly Catholic regions of a given country should have
lower suicide rates than predominantly Protestant regions of the
same country. When he looked at the appropriate suicide rates,
Durkheim found his expectations confirmed.

As another example, social researchers have recognized for a
long time that juvenile delinquency is higher in families where the
mother works than in families where the mother stays at home.
Such an observation lends itself to controversy, since it seems to
present a case against women's equal participation in the labor
force. Traditionalists have argued for years that "a woman's place
is in the home," and the statistics on juvenile delinquency suggest
some support for that view.

Social researchers have looked further into the matter, however, to ask why the higher delinquency rates occurred. Logically,
it seemed that children might be more likely to get in trouble if
they were not supervised after school—as might very well be the
case if the mother worked. This explanation suggested that any
adult supervision would reduce the likelihood of delinquency,
regardless of who did the supervising. Specifically, the explanation suggested that delinquency would be lower in families where
the mother worked but some other adult was available to supervise the children after school than in families where the mother
didn't work but wasn't home to supervise the children either. Subsequent observations showed the expectation to be correct: supervision was the key, not whether the mother worked.

You would do well to burn the phrase, "if that's the case,
then . . ." into your mind. Any time you think of or hear an explanation for anything, you should repeat the phrase, discover the
implications of the explanation, and then look to see if the implications are borne out by empirical observations. That precaution
can save you from countless embarrassments.

Consider the following example, which I've discussed in *The Practice of Social Research*. For decades, there has been concern over the problem of hunger in America and around the world. In response to that concern, in 1983 President Reagan appointed a thirteen-member Task Force on Food Assistance to find out if there was a hunger problem in the United States, and if so, what could be done about it.

Not surprisingly, the task force's job was deeply enmeshed in political issues. Concern for problems of poverty and hunger is traditionally more closely associated with the Democrats than with the Republicans, and the Reagan administration had been accused of caring less than most. The problems were also widely believed to affect blacks disproportionately more than whites, making hunger a racial as well as an economic issue.

In the midst of this situation, one member of the task force, Dr. George Graham, stirred up a political hornets' nest by publicly announcing his conclusion that the problem of malnutrition among blacks had been exaggerated. He was quoted as saying, "If you think that blacks as a group are undernourished, look around at the black athletes on television—they're a pretty hefty bunch."

Let's examine the logic of Graham's contention. If the heftiness of black athletes on television means that black Americans as a group are well nourished, then what else should be true? It would seem to follow, for example, that the existence of 300-pound sumo wrestlers would prove that the Japanese as a group are the best nourished people on earth. It would suggest the Japanese are a race of giants—certainly bigger than Americans, black or white. Such expectations would hardly be borne out by further empirical observation.

A similar misunderstanding emerges frequently in reference to "global warming" or "climate change." The conclusion shared by the vast majority of the scientific community is that the overall temperature of the planet is increasing in the long term. It has been further concluded that the increase in temperature is at least partly caused by human actions and that such an increase, if continued, represents a severe danger to life on the planet. Every now and then you will hear a "climate change denier" claim that a winter storm in some location disproves the overall contention. This assertion confuses weather (immediate) with climate (long-term) and confuses local conditions with those of the planet at large. As I write these words, the state of California is suffering a severe drought, despite the fact that it rained yesterday in Arkansas. Similarly, the fact that I had a big dinner last night does not disprove the existence of world hunger.

There are numerous other ways in which illogical reasoning can intrude into our understanding of the world we live in. Let me review a few problems that sometimes crop up in the context of social research.

Despite our discussions of probabilistic causation, people often feel justified in challenging the results of research by citing deviant cases. In response to the Durkheim study of suicide, for example, some people may counter by recalling a Catholic uncle who committed suicide or the report of a priest committing suicide. This case is then argued, incorrectly, as a sufficient disproof of the general conclusion that Catholics are less likely than Protestants to commit suicide. The problem here is that social scientific findings almost always describe the way things are in general, not in every particular.

It is always important to note whom a particular conclusion refers to. I suggest that no social scientist has ever learned anything that was true for the human race in general. Much of what American social scientists learn applies mostly to Americans, or perhaps to Western industrialized societies generally. Very often, what has been discovered applies far more narrowly than that.

The key to determining whom a particular conclusion applies to is to find whom the conclusion was drawn from. If a researcher has studied only sophomore psychology students at State University, you'd do well to ask whether the conclusions really apply to Armenian senior citizens in Arizona, to black pre-schoolers in Harlem, to Sherpa guides in the Himalayas, or to Middle Eastern terrorists.

Beliefs, values, and attitudes often get in the way of pure reason. Here's an example I find personally uncomfortable. Part of my continued interest in the issue of determinism is that it has a powerful, practical impact (via social science) on society. Most simply put, we have argued that many forms of deviance represent social problems rather than evil individuals. Thus, when a young, ill-educated black man in an urban ghetto holds up a liquor store, social scientists have been persuasive in showing the extent to which that act was the result of social forces the young man had no control over. We say he was a "product of his environment." In practical, societal terms, it could be argued that it wasn't really his fault; this position has in fact been argued effectively by social scientists, and I support it.

But I can't remember a single instance of a social scientist arguing that a Southern white klansman who burns a cross on the lawn of a black family is equally a product of his environment. We do not urge that he be seen as the victim of social forces he can't control. We do not urge that the court consider mitigating circumstances. I know I've never argued that point, even though logic makes the two situations equivalent. As suggested in Chapter 9, my inconsistency is purely a function of my sociopolitical bias in favor of racial and ethnic minorities.

I trust these few illustrations will point out that the research injunction to be reasonable is not as open-and-shut a matter as you might have thought. While we are perhaps all committed to being reasonable, we do not always live up to our ideals.

I close this discussion with two final points, one of which may be more troublesome than anything else I've written about in this book. First, the scientific commitment to logic and reason does not preclude nonlogical elements altogether. In fact, Robert Merton, a prominent American sociologist, popularized the term *serendipity* in reference to lucky coincidences or chance occurrences that can point us in the direction of important scientific discoveries. Any source of insight—including dreams, astrology, proverbs, and TV soap operas—is acceptable to a scientist, but it is only a source of insight; it doesn't prove anything by itself. Thus, you may dream about a cause of alienation or you may have a religious experience in which God tells you the cause of delinquency. Either is fine, but you must then look to see if the facts coincide with your insight.

Finally, it is important to recognize that our system of logical reasoning—a specific set of which is called *logical positivism*—is only a system of logic, not the ultimate truth. It is a tool to use in dealing with the world, not the world per se. In Chapter 3, I pointed out that rationality was not especially useful in connection with love, poetry, or sex. Now I raise a question about its even being the ultimate in understanding.

The way you and I reason about things is not omniscient. Recall the story about Galileo, Aristotle, and gravity. I said Galileo showed that Aristotle's position would hold two contradictory statements to be true. The two stones tied together would have to fall faster than the heavier stone by itself and slower than the heavier stone by itself. This couldn't happen, so of course Aristotle was wrong. That makes sense to me, as I'm sure it does to you.

Here's another way of looking at that situation. Our system of logic isn't very good with paradoxes. Statements are either true or false; they can't be both. Thus we come to a frustrating impasse with the Cretan who warns us that "All Cretans are liars." If the statement is true, then he was telling the truth rather than lying— thereby making his statement a lie. But if he lied, meaning Cretans tell the truth, then his statement must have been the truth rather than the lie that made it the truth in the first place.

Other systems of thought, such as Zen Buddhism and Taoism, are more adept at handling paradoxes. Zen koans—such as, "What is the sound of one hand clapping?"—purposely conflict with our most implicit notions of logical reason, to reveal to the student not so much new knowledge as new domains of knowing.

My purpose in these concluding remarks is not to suggest that Zen or Taoist ways of thinking are superior to our own. They are merely different, but their differences can point out that our own system of reasoning is like looking through lenses that add a particular tint to what we see. Any time you can see the tool with which you are seeing, you attain a profound breakthrough in your ability to see.

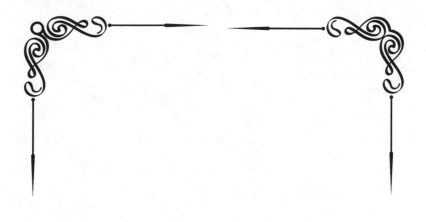

PART 5

THE SOCIAL CONTEXT OF RESEARCH

13

Scientific Closed-Mindedness

One of the cardinal virtues of science is open-mindedness. In fact, science and scientists have often gotten in trouble by challenging the closed-mindedness of the nonscientific. For example, when Galileo published his *Dialogue Concerning the Two Chief World Systems, Ptolemaic and Copernican*, supporting Copernicus's view that the earth revolved around the sun, he flew in the face of Catholic dogma and authority. Ultimately, he was forced to recant his views and acknowledge the Church's supremacy in such matters. Clearly, the Church was not a model of open-mindedness in that instance.

Similarly, people who are convinced that marijuana or pornography is mortally dangerous to everything sacred are unlikely to be moved by empirical research to the contrary. Those who insist that same-sex marriage will ruin marriage altogether are not bothered by their inability to explain how or give examples of marriages thus ruined. Nor are those who support capital punishment as a deterrent to murder likely to accept empirical research denying that it has that effect. Climate scientists have offended everyone who has investments in fossil fuels. And Darwin is still in trouble for saying creation took more than a week.

In contrast, science is committed to open-mindedness—to the constant challenge of old ideas and their replacement with new, presumably better ones. That's the ideal, but scientists sometimes fall short of the mark.

A number of years ago, I happened to come across a newspaper article entitled "Meditating Crime Away" about the alleged power of transcendental meditation (TM) in reducing crime. At first, I thought the article would talk about meditators' committing fewer crimes than other people do. What I discovered was quite different. The theme of the article was the assertion by TM spokespersons that, whenever a substantial number of people were meditating within a particular area, crime rates went down. In other words, even non-meditators stopped committing crimes when a lot of meditators were meditating in the vicinity.

That was only the beginning, however. The article went on to say that the TM people claimed other consequences of meditation on the surrounding society. Divorce rates decreased; marriage rates increased. Beer and cigarette consumption went down. The weather improved—more sunny days—and air pollution declined. It was the sort of newspaper article that usually sails past the periphery of my attention, landing in next week's *Sensational Revelations* (or something similar) at the supermarket checkout counter. Two things caught my attention, however.

First, the article contained data to support its contentions. For example, it reported that Rhode Island's suicide rate had decreased by 41.8 percent. Comments like that send a grappling hook into the heart of any incurable social researcher. I found myself asking a number of questions. Were those statistics trustworthy? Had there been a redefinition of suicide or a shift in the way suicide data were collected? What was the period covered by the data? Did it coincide with normal seasonal fluctuations? Did the decline in suicides refer to the whole state or only parts of it? Was it a uniform decline or were there regional variations?

These were the kinds of questions that occurred to me. There is something about being a methodologist that causes such questions to come to mind automatically. And the newspaper article didn't offer any answers to those questions.

I might have moved on at that point, but something else in the article caught my eye. One of the researchers reported that he had been having trouble getting his research results published: "One journal we sent to said the study was very well written and the statistics were impeccably done, but they just couldn't believe the theory behind it." The theory, it turned out, had something to do with the power of having more than 1 percent of a population meditating. At that point, a state change occurred, and the general social environment was transformed. I read it, but I didn't understand it and still don't.

Apparently, other people didn't get it either. When the San Francisco chief of police was asked about the decline in crime rate in an area targeted by TM for intense meditation, he replied,

"Are they claiming it went down because of their meditation? I'm just laughing. Who the hell knows why crime goes up or down? Put me down as a skeptic." A prominent social scientist responded similarly, saying it was difficult to deal with such claims because of their "patent absurdity," but he suggested that the TM researchers were "not deliberate cynical phonies."

At this point, I was not convinced by the results obtained by the TM researchers as reported in the article, but I was not convinced by the critics either. So, I called the TM researchers and asked for copies of their research reports.

The first report raised a number of methodological questions in my mind. Basically, it compared the crime rates (and other social indicators) of cities that had many TM meditators and those with few. Although cities with meditators had better statistics, I had some questions about the research design. What cities would have a higher percentage of meditators, I asked? It seemed to me that they would be generally younger, more affluent, more avant garde. Would those same characteristics also produce improved social characteristics with or without meditation? Were there other factors that might improve living conditions in a city, as well as making meditation popular? I made notes of my reservations about the conclusions drawn by the TM researchers.

As I proceeded to review the subsequent studies, most of the considerations I had had earlier were dealt with. The affluence of cities was controlled, for example, so it was possible to see if affluent communities with meditators did better than affluent communities without meditators. Each of the successive studies that I reviewed covered another of my methodological considerations. Together, they didn't handle all the possible problems, but they did tell me one thing: the researchers were genuinely committed to demonstrating the impact of TM in a conventional, empirical fashion. Later, when I consulted with local TM researchers, I confirmed that conclusion. Even though they were convinced of the rightness of their conclusions, they were committed to abiding by conventional norms of social research.

As far as I know, the research on the social impact of TM continues. I have lost touch with what has happened. I am able to contradict one of their assertions, however. TM executive Robert Roth said, "At this critical time in society the claims are too bold and the scientific research too impressive for it to be ignored." History has demonstrated again and again that no scientific research is too impressive to ignore if it contradicts the prevailing paradigm.

Think about how you are feeling about the discussion so far. In particular, when I began talking about the TM research, did you suspect that I was going to try to convince you that TM was a potent force for good in society? Did you wonder if I was going to be appropriately objective; were you a little wary about whether you could trust my judgment?

On the one hand, those concerns are essential for any scientist and are very useful for anyone who is exposed to reports of scientific research. Scientists are human, and they are capable of human frailties. Aside from having biases of various kinds, they sometimes just make mistakes. (I have never belonged to or participated in TM, by the way.)

At the same time, those concerns can be an impediment to your openness to new ideas. Similar concerns have produced opposition to every idea that is now established and accepted in science. To be effective, then, you need to walk a tightrope between being gullible and being closed-minded.

I found it useful to ask myself how I would feel if the TM research truly indicated what the researchers were saying it did. I found I was most concerned about being on the outside of something important. Suppose it turned out that TM really was making a powerful difference in the world. I had had numerous opportunities to become a meditator, and I had always turned them down. Like most humans, I justified those decisions at TM's expense. I told myself that I didn't need what they had to offer, so those who were meditating obviously needed something I didn't need.

The reasons we use to justify actions cause us to develop vested interests in the outcomes of other events. In this case, once I had chosen not to participate in TM and had justified my decision, it became important to me that TM be wrong. Now, if the research demonstrated that they were right all along, I'd feel like a physicist who had ridiculed Einstein's silly notions about time running faster or slower when we were moving. As I sat down to review the TM research, I realized I was looking through lenses colored by my previously unconscious opinions and vested interests in the matter. Being conscious of these allowed me to lift the lenses, at least part way, and see what was really there.

If TM research has suffered from closed-mindedness in the scientific community, astrology has probably had it worse. Despite the fact that many scientists of the past—Kepler, Newton, Tycho Brahe, and others—were supporters of astrology, modern scientists have been anything but. In 1975, with 43,000 people dying of starvation every day, with the constant threat of the planet being incinerated by a nuclear holocaust or slowly poisoned by pollution, 186 Nobel laureates took the time and trouble to sponsor a national media campaign to condemn astrology. The campaign was sponsored by the American Humanist Association, an organization committed to intellectual freedom. It didn't make any sense to me then, and it doesn't now.

A few years ago, I was asked to review a paper submitted for publication in an academic journal. Although I can't recall the journal, the title of the paper, or the authors' names, the paper was essentially an empirical test of astrology. They selected several well-known figures from history (e.g., Gandhi, Hitler) and determined their times and places of birth. These birth data (without names) were given to several astrologers who were asked to predict what kind of person each of the historical figures would have been. Would an astrologer have predicted, for example, that Hitler would become a great humanitarian?

The authors began by disclaiming any personal commitment to or belief in astrology, but they suggested that any discipline that had been around for 2,000 years probably deserved testing. That struck me as reasonable. As I recall, the analyses pointed to a statistically significant agreement between what astrologers would have predicted and how the subjects turned out, but the agreement was far from perfect. The authors suggested methodological adjustments that might be appropriate in any further studies on the subject.

In my view, the paper was a solid piece of research. It was well thought out, well written, and I suspected that many readers would find it interesting. I recommended publication. Later, I received copies of the comments of my fellow reviewers, both of whom recommended against publication. The main objection they had was that astrology had no place in a scientific journal. To publish the article would seem to lend credence to the validity of astrology. Again I was puzzled.

I myself neither believe nor disbelieve in astrology. I don't know much about it, so I feel it would be presumptuous of me to have an opinion. By astrological reckoning, I am a Capricorn—like Richard Nixon and my granddaughter. I've been told that Capricorns need to keep moving or they take root like trees, but that's about the extent of what I've heard about my sign. I did have my astrological chart prepared once by a friend who was a professional astrologer. I was curious to see if it would be of any value to me.

Some of what my friend said about people who were born where and when I was seemed pretty close to my own experience of what I was like; some of it didn't. Some of his predictions for the future seemed borne out by later events; others didn't; still others can't be judged yet. He told me to look for money to show up in October, and I'm still looking for it every October.

What interests me most about astrology is the resistance to it, especially among scientists. The resistance is particularly ironic, since it would be so easy to conduct a rigorous test of what astrologers purport to know. We could settle the matter once and for all, and those 186 Nobel laureates could then turn their attention to other matters. Here's how. Select a random sample of, say, 2,000 people from across the country. Ask each respondent for the date, time, and place of his or her birth. In addition, ask a number of questions regarding each respondent's beliefs, attitudes, and behaviors.

Once the data have been collected, engage a team of professional astrologers to classify the respondents on the basis of their birth data. Then have them predict how people in each astrological classification would respond regarding the beliefs, attitudes, and behaviors we asked about. For example, we might have asked people, "Do you believe in reincarnation?" My meager understanding of Capricorns suggests they would not be likely to hold an offbeat view like that, whereas my equally meager understanding of Aquarians (drawn solely from the musical, *Hair*) suggests they would be more likely to believe in it. In any event, real astrologers could make predictions of that order.

Once the predictions were made, the testing would be simple and straightforward. It would not be necessary for the astrologers to be right in all their predictions. After all, they do not claim we are totally controlled by the planets, but that the planets exert some influence on us. That kind of probabilistic causation is no stranger to social researchers, as we saw in Chapter 11. On the other hand, if the astrologers' predictions were no better than chance, that would pretty much invalidate the whole thing. A whole body of probability theory exists that would allow us to specify in advance what degree of accuracy in the predictions would be accepted as validating astrology and what would be accepted as invalidating it. This could be laid out in advance, as a way of avoiding disagreements, alibis, and debates later on.

As straightforward as this test would be, I doubt that it will ever occur. After all, the 186 Nobel laureates did not propose a definitive test or an opportunity to demonstrate the invalidity of astrology. They simply wanted it eradicated.

These two examples are by no means the only exceptions to an otherwise unblemished record of scientific open-mindedness. In 1969, Arthur Jensen initiated a national controversy by publishing research findings in the *Harvard Educational Review* suggesting that blacks had intrinsically lower IQs than whites. While some researchers later made telling methodological criticisms of Jensen's research, most of the opposition he received on college campuses was far from scientific. He was shouted down at speaking engagements. Demands were made for the elimination of Jensenism—strikingly similar to eighteenth-century calls for the elimination of Jennerism, referring to the smallpox vaccine developed by Edward Jenner.

Here's a more esoteric example. Edward Wilson is a Harvard zoologist and is generally acknowledged as the founder of sociobiology, which he has defined briefly as "the systematic study of the biological basis of all forms of social behavior, including sexual and parental behavior, in all kinds of organisms, including humans." The sociobiological view contradicts much of what social scientists have done throughout the history of social science. Where we might look to socialization or to peer pressure to explain a particular kind of behavior, Wilson suggests the behavior is simply a result of biological factors.

As you can imagine, sociobiology has not escaped the attention of social scientists. Again, some have developed powerful methodological critiques of the sociobiological paradigm, but most of the response has been of a different sort. Wilson has been condemned as antifeminist, for example, because of the implications of his paradigm for sex roles. The American Anthropological Association, at a national convention, voted officially to condemn sociobiology—not to test it, but to condemn it.

This conversation could go on at much greater length, but I trust the point of the chapter has been made. Nonetheless, I am uneasy about having raised this issue. For one thing, I am concerned that my criticism of scientific resistance to a particular person or paradigm will be interpreted as support on my part for that person or paradigm. Thus, I want to be clear that (1) I am not yet able to judge the validity of the TM research; (2) I have no opinion as to the validity or invalidity of astrology; (3) I feel there are important methodological flaws in the Jensen report; and (4) I tend to oppose sociobiology for reasons of being out of work if it's true.

My second concern about this discussion is that it may look like another debunking of the sacred cow, science. There have been any number of articles published to show that scientists aren't as cool and rational as they pretend. Most such discussions make no positive contribution; they seem aimed simply at dragging science down, rather than supporting scientists to live even closer to our scientific ideals. The latter is my purpose in this chapter.

As humans, we are often narrow-minded, prejudiced, and stupid. And yet, we have something more powerful than that: as if in obedience to some mystic creed, we scientists are ultimately open to new ideas. Sometimes we hate that commitment. Sometimes we violate the creed. And yet we always reassert it eventually. It's like some ethereal music calling us home. We are driven to see what really lies beyond the next mountaintop, regardless of what we hope is there. The scientific community is perhaps our best hope for open-mindedness, and I want it to be even more potent in that regard.

14

Value-Free Science?

In Chapter 2, I suggested that objectivity was inherently impossible. In this chapter, I take up a related issue. Whether or not scientists can be truly objective in their inquiries, it is widely agreed that their subjective values should not interfere with their research. Two researchers—one Democrat and one Republican—should be able to conduct independent studies to determine whether, on the average, Democrats or Republicans have more education, and they should reach the same conclusion. (Republicans have more education.) It is in this sense, perhaps, that science is sometimes called *value free*.

The question I raise in this chapter is whether individual researchers should be value free with regard to what they study. How do you feel, for example, about the American Tobacco Institute conducting research on whether cigarettes cause cancer? How about big petroleum companies studying whether global warming is real and whether it is caused by humans? What do you think when a political candidate's campaign staff conducts a poll and announces that its candidate is favored by the majority of voters?

You probably feel these forms of research should be permitted under the law, but you may also take a rather jaundiced view of their results. What is the probability that the American Tobacco Institute will publish research results showing that tobacco is hazardous to your health? It's about the same as the probability that oil and coal interests will claim they are warming the planet or the probability that a political campaign staff will announce that their candidate is going down the tubes.

In cases where the researchers have such a vested interest in the research results, certain research outcomes are inconceivable. As a result, we greet their research reports with the thought that:

1. they have used research techniques that biased the results in their favor;
2. they have conducted repeated studies, with varied results, and they are only publishing the ones they liked; or
3. both of the above.

We are more trusting when the Surgeon General reports on cigarette smoking, when university researchers study climate change, or when an independent polling agency tells us which candidate is currently preferred. Presumably, these sources do not have as much of a vested interest in the outcome of those particular issues.

This is not to say that we feel the Surgeon General is inherently more trustworthy than the American Tobacco Institute. We might feel a little less trusting if the Surgeon General came to congressional budget hearings with research findings indicating that office had spent its budget more effectively than any other government agency.

Notice, however, that having a vested interest doesn't disprove research results. Maybe the Surgeon General's office is, by some reasonable definition, the most fiscally responsible agency in government. Some agency deserves that honor. If the Surgeon General's office were the one, that fact would not be invalidated just because the Surgeon General's office was the one to discover it. Still, its obvious vested interest would signal us to proceed with caution.

This situation is similar to the discussion of TM research in Chapter 13. That the research was being conducted by people who were personally participating in TM was reason for extra caution. We need not assume, though, that people with vested interests will consciously lie or cheat: there are ample opportunities to affect the outcome of research without consciously trying to.

Consider the following hypothetical situation, and judge whether it seems appropriate conduct for a social researcher. Let's suppose you became deeply concerned about the danger of global warming and decided the development of renewable energy sources was essential to the survival of life on the planet. Accordingly, you decide to create a climate of opinion on your college campus in favor of research on renewable energy.

Since you've been trained as a social scientist, you begin by conducting an opinion survey to find out how the campus community feels about global warming and renewable energy. You find (let's say) that the majority of people on campus deny the reality of global warming. Instead of publishing the results of the survey, you analyze the nature of people's denial. Based on what you can determine about why people deny the reality of global warming, you launch a public information campaign to counteract their views.

After a few months, you conduct another survey to measure opinions about global warming. Now, the campus is about evenly divided. Again, you keep the results of the survey quiet and use what you have learned to design and launch another information campaign. When you conduct another survey later on, a solid majority of people on campus are convinced on the reality of global warming and are in support of developing renewable energy sources.

What do you think? Would that be appropriate behavior for a social researcher? Would you feel any differently if the purpose was to bring campus opinion to oppose abortion? Or to support a woman's right to choose? What if the researcher's purpose was to gain campus support for the American Nazi Party or for the Communist Party U.S.A.? How about getting support for the Tea Party or the Green Party?

If none of those possibilities seems appropriate to you, suppose the researcher's purpose was to gain support for famine relief or to eliminate racial prejudice? Your opinion is probably somewhat dependent on whether you agree or disagree with the researcher's purpose. That's only natural.

Each of us has personal biases, and these show up in our views of value-free science. We're not particularly concerned when we find that a cancer researcher hates cancer or that an environmental researcher is personally opposed to pollution. So why are we concerned when we learn that someone studying religious behavior is personally opposed to religion or that someone studying capitalism in America is an outspoken critic of capitalism?

In part, the distinctions reflect our personal and shared biases; but there is more to it than that. Probably the cancer researcher's hating cancer will not affect his or her research results. This is not to say that a given researcher won't come to believe in a new cure or a new theory and start ignoring contradictory evidence. That is all the more likely to the extent that the researcher's ego becomes bound up with the research. When people start calling the new theory the Babbie Theory, you shouldn't count on my being completely unbiased about it from then on.

But in cases like that, the hatred of cancer is not the cause of bias and error.

Personal biases become more problematic when research outcomes have their impact through the medium of public opinion. Consider the case of the antichurch atheist studying religion in America. Suppose the researcher discovers that church members, on the average, contribute more to charity than do those who do not attend church. The finding in and of itself has no impact on anything (especially since the researcher is unlikely to become religious). Only when it is communicated does it have an impact. If people know that church members contribute more to charity, perhaps that knowledge will increase the esteem in which organized religion is held in America. In view of this, the researcher might be tempted to suppress the finding.

There is no parallel to this in the case of the cancer researcher who hates cancer. Suppose an experiment shows that a new treatment has no effect on cancer. Concealing that fact will not do any damage to cancer. If every man, woman, and child in America knows that the treatment doesn't work, cancer will gain nothing. In other words, there is no public opinion factor.

Let's suppose the antichurch religion researcher is sufficiently biased to set all scientific scruples aside in order to damage churches. The skillful use of some questionable research techniques produces findings that reflect badly indeed on organized religion. The researcher publishes those findings, is vague about the methodology involved, and generally makes it difficult for other researchers to critique the findings. Even if the research is subsequently discredited, the initially published findings may have had an impact through the medium of public opinion. Some people will have become more negative toward organized religion as a consequence of what they believed was shown by scientific research.

So far in this discussion, I've focused on the potential dangers of researchers being personally involved in what they are studying, but there is another side to the issue as well. The priest who wants to study religion, for example, begins with a wealth of information about the subject that is not available to other researchers. The same would be true of astrologers who wanted to test the efficacy of astrology. And capitalist leaders know a lot about capitalism.

Researchers who are hired by people with a vested interest in the subject under study sometimes have a similar advantage. Let's suppose you were hired by the Surgeon General's office to determine how responsibly it spent its budget. Even though you might not have any special knowledge about the office's operations going in, you'd probably be given access to information not readily available to outsiders.

Extensive information through personal involvement, as I've been describing it, is an important resource for analysis, and it can also be the basis for special insights as well. Anthropologists have long recognized that going native is a two-way street. On the one hand, the anthropologist who strips naked and begins living on bugs, roots, and berries may lose "objectivity" about the people under study. Yet, actually living the subject matter in that way can also reveal things that an outsider would never see or feel.

Thus, there are both benefits and dangers in having researchers personally involved in what they study. Here are some suggestions on how to recognize the dangers inherent in a researcher's being too personally involved in his or her subject matter.

First and foremost, keep most of your attention on the quality of the methodological design and execution of the research—and on the clarity with which it is reported. Regardless of the particular research technique employed—survey, experiment, field observations, or whatever—be sure that the researcher has used the technique properly. If members of a church are being surveyed, for example, has a proper sample been selected? Are the questions proper ones for a survey? If an experiment has been conducted, does it include control groups or quasi-controls?

Second, be sure that methodological details have been reported responsibly. If you cannot tell what kind of sampling has been undertaken or what questions were asked, that should immediately warn you that the research was not very well done. Thus, for example, you should be cautious about the pro-astrology researcher who reports that the astrologer's predictions were far more accurate than would have been expected by chance, without telling you exactly how much more accurate the predictions were and what standard was used in that determination.

Third, check the thoroughness of the analysis of data. Having reached an initial conclusion that supports his or her personal values, does the researcher play devil's advocate in looking for alternative explanations? A superficial analysis of data may signify undue influence of personal values.

The suggestions I've made for guarding against researchers who are too personally involved in their subject matter apply to the evaluation of research in general. You should be cautious about any research that uses improper techniques, is not adequately reported, or is superficial in its analyses. Researchers may err in consequence of being untrained, lazy, stupid, or just human. Error can also point to the impact of personal biases. Ultimately, you don't need to know why a piece of research should not be trusted—it's sufficient to know you can't trust it.

In addition to these warning signs, sometimes the researcher's language can point to the undue impact of personal biases. Reporting that church members gave more money to charity than those who weren't church members did, for example, is a straightforward account of a research finding. Stating the matter in value-laden terms ("Church members are more generous than other people") may point to bias, especially if the assertion goes beyond the facts ("Church members care more about the suffering of others").

While you should pay attention to the use of nonscientific language, you should avoid being too strict in that regard. Social scientists have produced some of the worst prose in the history of the English language (I can't speak for other languages), and I think this is largely due to a concern for sounding scientific. Therefore, you should welcome an interesting, understandable, well-written report that is faithful to the data and the analyses.

In this chapter, I've mostly talked about the need for you to guard against the personal biases of other researchers. No less important is the need to keep yourself in check. It's perhaps more important, since you're in an excellent position to make a difference in that respect. I can illustrate this best through personal examples.

Much of my early research focused on the sociology of religion. While I was quite religious as a young person, I had become much less so by the time I began studying religion sociologically. When asked about my interest in studying religion, I would reply that it was a powerful social institution and that I wanted to understand more about how it worked.

Many of my colleagues in the sociology of religion were personally involved in religion, as clergy or as laypeople. To tell the truth, I felt basically superior to them. After all, I was discovering the naturalistic explanations for something they believed was mystical and supernatural. They were still stuck in something I had grown out of, as though they still believed in Santa Claus. When I finally gave up my research on religion, I explained that I had learned everything I had wanted to know about it. I was too smart to say I had learned everything worth knowing, but there was an element of that in my view of the matter.

Today, looking back on that experience, I can see that I probably could have learned a few more things about religion. While I have not been born again nor even resumed attending church, I can recognize my earlier point of view about religion as merely a point of view, just as my more religious colleagues had their points of view. Moreover, each of those points of view influenced what we saw—mine no less than anyone else's.

For my PhD dissertation, I undertook a national survey of medical school faculty members. The project had been proposed by Dr. Otto Guttentag, a medical philosopher at the San Francisco Medical Center. I was hired as a research assistant to support his work by virtue of my training in social research.

At issue in the research was whether the growth of science in medicine was undercutting the human qualities of medical care. More to the point, were scientifically oriented doctors more impersonal and less responsible in their care of patients? While I had no special training or experience in the field of medicine, that didn't prevent me from having opinions in the matter. It seemed pretty obvious to me that science made medicine more detached and impersonal—and more power to it! I thought medicine should be like that. Given the choice between a warm and kindly old fuddy-duddy and somebody who was efficient, competent, and impersonal, I knew who I wanted. As a consequence, I entered the project expecting to show how wonderful science was in medicine.

I wasn't as conscious of that point of view as I am now, but it was definitely an implicit position that influenced my whole approach to the research. Moreover, I felt that Guttentag represented the other side of the issue, that he favored the nonscientific physician. Thus, the project was to be, in part, a contest between the forces of the past (Guttentag) and the forces of the future (me).

My implicit point of view was sufficiently entrenched that it took me about half the period of the project to hear what Guttentag was actually saying. He really wanted to find out if scientific orientations were undercutting the human qualities of medicine, and he particularly wanted to know if medicine could be both scientific and humane. I finally comprehended this when my initial data analyses failed to come out as I had anticipated.

I had begun by developing a measure of whether faculty members were more interested in medical science (for example, interested in articles on the rationale behind new treatments) or in patient care (for example, interested in articles on the effectiveness of treatments). For the sake of simplicity, I'll call these two groups the *scientists* and the *non-scientists*, respectively. Next, I quickly demonstrated that the scientists were more likely to engage in medical research than were the non-scientists.

The obvious next step was to show that the scientists were less likely than the non-scientists to engage in patient care, either at their university or in private practice. But, to my surprise, there was no difference! The scientists were seeing just as many patients as the non-scientists. I recovered from this surprise with the assumption that there would be a real difference in the nature of the care they provided patients.

A number of questions in our questionnaire asked whether the respondents would take personal responsibility for their patients in various situations, as opposed to delegating the responsibility to house staff members. Suppose a patient died, for example. Would the faculty member in charge personally meet with the patient's family or delegate that job to an intern? Or, if there were a medical emergency on the weekend, did the faculty member want to be called personally or let the house staff handle it? It seemed obvious to me that the scientists would delegate responsibility, since that fit in with the idea of specialization, the division of labor, and other modern approaches to life.

As it turned out, the scientists and non-scientists did not differ in the extent to which they maintained or delegated responsibility for their patients. Neither did they differ on issues of medical ethics regarding experimentation. Eventually, I was able to see that scientific and humane medicine were not incompatible. Some faculty members were scientifically inclined, and others weren't. Some of the scientists were warm and compassionate, while others weren't; and the same was true of the non-scientists. Science did not make medicine cold and impersonal. I had been prevented from seeing the nature of the relationship between scientific and humane medicine because of my own bias in favor of science—in what I took to be an inescapable dichotomy. Fortunately, the data proved a stern taskmaster, and I was eventually forced to see things differently.

As a final example, I was once asked to analyze a set of data collected in a national survey of graduates of the Erhard Training Seminars (*est*) training, a program of personal transformation. The request came from the organization that sponsored the *est* training. The questionnaire had asked respondents a variety of questions regarding the experience of taking the training and any benefits or problems they had experienced afterward. While the data had been collected by an independent research team, the results had never been published. That's what I was now asked to do.

My first analyses of the data showed overwhelmingly positive reports. The vast majority of respondents said they enjoyed the training and reported improvements in their relationships with family and friends, productivity in work and school, mental health, and so forth. Since I had taken the training myself and had enjoyed it, I was not surprised by the research results.

As I looked further into my feelings, however, I noticed I was more than not surprised; I was also pleased and relieved. In fact, I took the results as a vindication of my having taken the training, which had sometimes been criticized by academics who hadn't taken it. Once I became aware of the extent to which I was responding to the results out of my own biases, I consciously reversed my analytical orientation and began to play the devil's advocate as strongly as I could.

Were the positive reports of the training the result of a self-fulfilling prophecy? Did people report benefiting only because they thought they would? Were the respondents really qualified to judge whether they had benefited or suffered from the training?

As I considered the implications of these critiques, I found ways of testing each within the data available. In regard to the respondents' qualifications to judge, for example, I asked whether the average person could tell whether their mental health had improved or worsened. After all, that was the sort of judgment we usually leave to professional therapists. So I looked at the responses of the therapists in the sample, and I found that they were as positive about their experiences as were the rest of the respondents in the sample. On the issue of productivity, I focused on engineers and other professionals I felt might be relatively capable of judging.

For me, this was a happy research experience. In order to guard against my own biases, I was far more diligent and imaginative than normal in my data analyses, and that report remains one of those I am proudest of. I hope you will see in this example the possibility of turning a potential danger into an opportunity.

Individual scientists cannot be value free, any more than we can be truly objective. All of us have values, beliefs, opinions, biases, expectations, and other points of view that influence what we see. Sometimes you can recognize how your values are affecting your research and take steps to counteract such influences.

Sometimes you can do no more than acknowledge what your points of view may be. You should be most cautious when you think you have no biases operating, since you surely have some.

If no individual scientist can be value free, there is somewhat more hope for science as a collective enterprise. With individual scientists checking up on each other (peer review) and pointing out each other's individual biases and other shortcomings, the whole of science is indeed more than the sum of its parts.

At the same time, science collectively has its own biases, in the form of dominant paradigms. Thus, while the scientific community as a collective may see the foibles of individual members, it has more difficulty seeing its group biases; that becomes the task of individual members who are willing to challenge prevailing views.

15

⁓⊙⊙⊙⊱

The First Science

Years ago, as chair of the sociology department at the University of Hawaii, I had the pleasure of leading a special kind of graduate seminar. I forget the official title of the course, but it was informally known as "Meet Your Local Professor." The course was created for the benefit of entering graduate students, to give them some exposure to the entire department faculty so they could begin deciding whom they might like to study with, who they wanted to have on their dissertation committees, and the like.

The course was organized in a television interview show format. Once a week, I would present one or two faculty members to the class. To get things rolling, I would begin with an informal interview. One of the first questions I usually asked was, "How did you come to be a sociologist?" As you might imagine, not all members of the faculty started out planning to be sociologists. As you might not imagine, only one out of twenty had entered college with the intention of being a sociologist. All the others had planned to major in biology, physics, math, or some other field.

My own experience was perhaps typical. As I mentioned in the reflexive introduction, I arrived at college planning to be an engineer, but Harvard didn't have an engineering school at that time, so I switched my plans to physics. After great difficulty in German and calculus, I happened by chance into a course in cultural anthropology and my future was reshaped in a good way.

My purpose in these comments is to indicate that sociology and the other social sciences do not necessarily measure up to our conventional images of science. Some people are inclined to put the science part of social science in italics or quotes, and social scientists are sometimes a bit defensive in asserting our claim to the title.

In this concluding chapter, I address the question: are the social sciences really sciences? Since I am the most familiar with sociology, my discussion will focus rather closely on that particular field, though I suspect my comments apply to the other social sciences as well. Thus, when I talk about sociology, I mean to include such allied fields as anthropology, psychology, political science, economics, and geography.

Let me start by answering *yes* to the question. Not only is sociology clearly a science in my view, but I further assert that it may deserve the title of *the first science*.

My basic contention is that the so-called sciences like physics, biology, and chemistry have not been sufficiently challenging to have developed into full sciences. Each has contributed to the development of science in general, but none has provided an opportunity for science to mature fully as an approach to understanding. Fifty years from now, we'll look back on the history of sociology (and the other social sciences) and say, "That's how we finally came to see the possibility of science in its fullness."

Martin Trow, a sociologist of education, once spoke of an irony in the use of survey research methods in the study of education. He began by noting that the educational setting was ideally suited for conducting surveys. Sampling was no problem, since there were lists of students, and students could be reached easily. In fact, they could often be asked to fill out questionnaires in the classroom, under controlled conditions. They were literate and accustomed to filling out forms. All of this, moreover, made surveys in schools easy and inexpensive.

Wasn't it ironic, he continued, that survey research had not produced any profound discoveries in the study of education? He concluded that the problem was precisely that survey research was so easy to do in the educational setting. Researchers seldom had to make compromises in designing research; hence they didn't have to look very deeply into the logic of research design per se. As a consequence, research was routine and unimaginative.

By contrast, researchers who were unable to get neat lists of the populations they wanted to study had to reflect on the nature of populations and sampling. Given that ideal sampling designs were impossible, what compromises would offer the best approximations of what was needed? Outside the classroom, moreover, many people refused to participate in surveys. What effect did that have on the validity of conclusions drawn entirely from answers given by people who were willing to participate? What adjustments could be made to accommodate any biases that might result from the refusals? This issue has become increasingly taxing in recent years, when response rates in telephone surveys have been declining.

What Trow observed about the uses of survey research in studying education, I suggest, is true with regard to the natural sciences. Daniel Suits, an economist, once suggested that instead of distinguishing between the "hard" and "soft" sciences, as is commonly done, we should distinguish between the "hard" and "easy" sciences. Moreover, in Suits's classification, the social sciences were the hard ones; the natural sciences were the easy ones.

If you've ever studied the theory and methods of sampling in the social sciences, you know that it can be a very complicated task. If you have ever drawn a real sample under normal social research conditions, you realize that sampling is a far subtler matter than it may appear in a textbook discussion.

While a graduate student at Berkeley, I was given the job of selecting a sample of households in Oakland, California, to be used in a study of unemployment and poverty. If the overall unemployment rate in Oakland exceeded 8 percent, the city would be eligible for federal funds. Our job was to determine what the city's unemployment rate was and to make our determination in such a way that the federal government would accept our findings.

Gaining acceptance of our findings in Washington hinged on a number of factors. For example, it would be necessary to define and measure unemployment in a way that would compare with standardized procedures. Was a full-time student considered unemployed? How about handicapped people? Should we count wealthy heiresses who neither needed nor desired to work? What about people in the military? Hundreds of questions like these needed to be answered appropriately.

Sampling was another cornerstone for the acceptance of the findings. If we ended up calculating that more than 8 percent of the people in our sample were unemployed, could that be taken as a true representation of the whole city? Who was "the city"? Did Oakland include residents who were away on vacations at the time of the study? How about those away for tours in the military or for study at college? On the other hand, did it include visitors from elsewhere? How about those who were trying to make up their minds about moving? What about sailors from New York, temporarily stationed at the Port of Oakland?

Whatever decisions were made in regard to questions like these, there was no adequate list of the residents of Oakland. It would be necessary to approximate such a listing. We decided to select a sample of census blocks from among the 2,000 or so that the city had been divided into. Once we had selected a representative sample of blocks, we would go into the field to make lists of all the households on each of the selected blocks. Then, we would select samples of households from each of those blocks. Finally, we would interview the residents of each selected household.

I'll spare you the complex statistics that went into determining how many blocks to select and how many households to select from each block. The determining factor, however, was the chance Oakland officials were willing to take that the survey would underestimate unemployment by a big enough margin to lose the federal funding—assuming the city really qualified for it. The decision was to select 700 blocks and 5 households from each block, for a total of 3,500 households.

How would you select a sample of 700 blocks from the 2,000 constituting the city? You might consider a map and 700 darts, but that wouldn't generally be judged appropriate. To create our strategy, we had to reconsider the purpose of sampling in general and then find methods that would best serve that purpose. Simply put, we wanted a sample of blocks that had the same characteristics as all the blocks as a whole. In other words, the blocks we selected should be just like the ones we omitted. This suggested a strategy called *stratification*.

If we could arrange the census blocks in homogeneous groups, it wouldn't matter too much which block was selected from any particular group. The key was that the blocks in any given group had to have the same characteristics. But in what characteristics should they be alike? Once again, this required a reconsideration of the logic of sampling. We decided on such variables as size of block, percentage of nonwhite/white residents, percentage of renters/owners, average home value or rent, and similar characteristics. Our decisions were based in part on knowing what census data were available for describing the blocks.

Other considerations also needed to be handled in the selection of a representative sample in Oakland. What difference would it make if the descriptive census data for some blocks were out of date? What if the size or racial composition of a block had changed since the census data were compiled, for example? What steps could be taken to remedy such changes? Since we planned to select five households from each selected block, what could be done with blocks that turned out to have fewer than five households altogether? How should we account for people who refused to be interviewed?

Overall, the selection of 3,500 households took about two months, and I've only touched on a few of the questions that needed to be answered and problems that needed to be solved. I trust I've gone into enough detail to give you at least some idea of the extent to which we needed to discover anew the purpose and nature of representative samples. That, in turn, required that we keep reviewing the basic implications of variations in the characteristics of units under study.

By contrast to what was required to sample households in Oakland, consider a team of chemical researchers who want to conduct experiments on the nature of iron. Do they lose any sleep over the need to make a list of all the iron in the world or go over the best method for sampling from the whole? No, they merely send a lab assistant down to the corner chemical supply store to get three dollars' worth of iron. (They call it Fe just to impress people with how scientific they are.) Or consider the physiologists who want to study the characteristics of human blood. They'll probably want to get some A, B, AB, and O type blood. Other than that, they hardly need to be more discriminating than the average vampire.

The point is that, while some other scientific disciplines deal with the idea of sampling, social scientists have contributed more to our understanding of the logic of sampling and practical techniques for selecting samples than all the other sciences combined.

The various discussions of definition and measurement in earlier chapters provide another instance of social science having to be far more sophisticated than the "easy" sciences. Any college freshman can grasp the meaning of distance, mass, velocity, and acceleration. But compare those measurements with such everyday social science variables as alienation, prejudice, authoritarianism, class consciousness, and so forth. The difficulty inherent in measuring such social science variables requires a highly sophisticated appreciation of what's involved in making distinctions, specifying concepts, testing the validity and reliability of measures, and deciding related issues—matters that do not necessarily come to mind when the measuring is easy.

We've also looked at the recursive aspect of the social sciences. What we learn about human social life can end up changing the accuracy of what we learn. Thus, if we conduct a simple investigation to find out what county in America has the lowest unemployment rate and publish our findings, within weeks that county would no longer have the lowest unemployment rate because hundreds or thousands of job seekers would have flocked there.

There are some parallels to the natural sciences—for example, when we find the cause of a disease, we take steps to cure it. However, the recursive quality is far more complex and fundamental within the social sciences. Whatever we learn, we learn about ourselves; research itself is a social process. Once again, the social sciences, by their very nature, simply require a far more sophisticated view of science to get their work done.

And don't forget our earlier discussion of determinism and freedom. The subjects for study in sociology have volition or *agency*. There are usually multiple causes for whatever choices they make—and no two people have the same set of multiple factors causing their choices. Imagine iron filings have a choice as to whether they would accept the magnet's invitation for a pickup. Each filing would consider different factors. And ultimately filings would choose to be picked up while others chose to lie on the table and wait for a better offer. Imagine having to calculate the probability of iron filings choosing to be picked up.

Causation in sociology is always probabilistic, rarely if ever 100 percent certain. To be sure, some natural scientists have to deal with probabilities (in genetics, for example) but not to the extent that sociologists do, though quantum physicists may be getting a taste of what sociologists have been dealing with from the beginning.

By no means do I want to suggest in these remarks that social scientists have mastered all the complex issues of science I've been discussing, or even that social scientists are sufficiently aware of all those issues. To suggest that would be to contradict most of what has already been said in this book. After all, the social sciences are very young in comparison with the natural sciences.

Still, there is no question in my mind that the full development of science will be realized in the social sciences for the reasons of apparent adversity I discussed. It is not a question of whether the social sciences are or can be scientific. We are well on the road to becoming the first science.

Afterword

I conclude this book by returning to a couple of topics covered in earlier chapters: the idea of being objective and value free. These concepts have applications well beyond the social sciences, and what we have seen in the earlier discussions may help in the application of those concepts elsewhere.

There are many places in modern society where we expect objectivity. In this sense, it can be seen as the opposite of prejudice or bias. Thus, we expect an employer to treat all employees "fairly," without playing favorites on the basis of such things as race, religion, gender, sexual orientation, and so on. Moreover, we expect the same objectivity in restaurants, hotels, medical clinics, and many other places.

As we move into the realm of government, this expectation seems even more important. We expect it from police, firefighters, voting registrars, welfare workers, and all other government officials. Whenever police appear to be discriminating on the basis of race, for example, that often results in protest in the streets.

One way we approach this issue rests on the expectation that likes will favor likes. So if the entire police force is white, racial minorities in the community may worry that they will be discriminated against. Similarly, women may worry when an all-male legislative committee determines whether women should have the rights to contraception and abortion. In all cases like these, those suspected of bias claim to be objective.

This issue took an interesting turn in 2009, when nominee, now Associate Justice, Sonia Sotomayor spoke of adding the perspectives of a "wise Latina" to the U.S. Supreme Court. The entire conservative wing of American politics leaped on her remark.

When pressed by the Senators, she acknowledged that all her various characteristics, gender, ethnicity, and others would have an inevitable effect on how she saw things, but she assured the Senate that she would not allow such factors to rule her judgments.

A starkly contrasting view had been offered four years earlier when John Roberts was questioned by the Senate in his hearings. Justices had to be objective, he said. Like umpires, they simply "called ball and strikes." Once on the bench, of course, Roberts' decisions have been predictably aligned with his conservative points of view, which I'm sure he does not recognize as points of view: just a matter of balls and strikes.

For many people, the established status quo is implicitly neutral and non-biased. Anything that varies from the status quo—women, Hispanics, or blacks, for example—are, by this definition, biased. Mature, white men are not recognized as a category: they represent the lack of category. They are vanilla.

Reflecting on this imagery during the Sotomayor hearings led me to compose the following piece for the campus newspaper. With the demographic changes occurring in the United States, I hope you will find this of interest, regardless of your "flavor."

Growing Up Vanilla

I remember the day I first realized I was a heterosexual. Well, actually, I don't remember that. I suppose one day I learned about homosexuals and decided I wasn't one. I was "normal," with no need to adjust, adapt, or cope with anything.

I remember the day my parents explained to me that I was white. Well, actually, they never brought it up. Growing up in Vermont, it was years before I discovered there were non-white people. After I had moved to New Hampshire, during my high school years, two black students from Connecticut came to attend our school. I remember that the boy was good at athletics and was generally liked. The girl was a little outspoken and abrasive, and people used to wish she were more like the boy. He was nice. On the whole, however, they were interruptions in the "regular."

It was the same thing with being a Protestant Christian. Though I heard about people who would "Jew you down" (talk you into a lower price) in a business transaction, I had no idea that there was a religious reference involved—or that there were other religions. (I knew people might "gyp" you, but I had no idea that comment was related to gypsies—although I had some image of them.)

When I was in elementary school, I knew one family that was "Catholic," whatever that was, and they went to church in another town. That seemed weird to me, although I had no idea what it meant.

At some point, I learned that girls were "different." They had special deficits and special needs. They were human but they weren't exactly boys. They were missing some parts.

Whereas many people have had to learn to deal with being "different," typically in ways that cause them problems in our society, I grew up vanilla, with none of that. To be sure, I was poor, but so was nearly everyone I knew. The few rich people were different, too, but I suppose I would have been willing to cope with their marginal status. As far as I knew, I was absolutely ordinary. Some other people might have special, different, unusual flavors. But I was vanilla.

Then one day I realized that vanilla ice cream was a *flavor*. It wasn't neutral or plain. Similarly, my own vanilla status was also a special flavor; it wasn't "just the way things are" or the way things are "supposed to be." I grew up in a culture with particular characteristics that had all the same elements and meanings as the cultures and characteristics of other people: gays, blacks, Jews, women, and so on.

Many, many years later, I was shocked to learn that my "vanilla" status was a distinct minority in the world at large. Not only were there people different from me—I was outnumbered. There are more of "them" than "us."

Hope they like vanilla.

Bibliography

Arbesman, S. (2012). *The half-life of facts: Why everything we know has an expiration date.* New York: Current Hardcover (Penguin Random House).

Babbie, E. (1985). *You can make a difference.* New York: St. Martin's Press.

Berger, P. L., & Luckman, T. (1966). *The social construction of reality: A treatise in the sociology of knowledge.* Garden City, NY: Doubleday.

Broad, W., & Wade, N. (1982). *Betrayers of the truth: Fraud and deceit in the halls of science.* New York: Simon and Schuster.

Habermas, J. (1979). *Communication and the evolution of society.* London: Heinemann.

Horowitz, I. L. (ed.). (1967). *The rise and fall of project Camelot.* Cambridge, MA: MIT Press.

Jaynes, J. (1976). *The origin of consciousness in the breakdown of the bicameral mind.* Boston: Houghton Mifflin.

Kahane, H. (1980). *Logic and contemporary rhetoric: The use of reason in everyday life.* Belmont, CA: Wadsworth.

Kaplan, A. (1964). *The conduct of inquiry: Methodology for behavioral science.* New York: Harper and Row.

Kuhn, T. (1970). *The structure of scientific revolution.* Chicago: University of Chicago Press.

Mannheim, K. (1936). *Ideology and utopia.* London: Routledge & Kegan Paul.

Morris, C. W. (ed.). (1934). *Mind, self & society from the standpoint of a social behaviorist* (Works of George Herbert Mead, Vol. 1). Chicago: University of Chicago Press.

Piaget, J. (1954). *The construction of reality in the child.* New York: Basic Books.

Poynard, T., Munteanu, M., Ratziu, V., Benhamou, Y., Di Martino, V., Taieb, J., & Opolon, P. (2002). Truth survival in clinical research: An evidence-based requiem? *Annals of Internal Medicine, 136*(12), 888–895.

Simmel, G. (1968). *The conflict in modern culture, and other essays* (K. P. Etzkorn, trans.). New York: Teachers College Press, Columbia University.

Tang, R. (2008). Citation characteristics and intellectual acceptance of scholarly monographs. *College & Research Libraries, 69*(4), 356–369.

U.S. Census Bureau. (2012). *Statistical abstract of the United States.* Washington, DC: U.S. Government Printing Office.

Weber, M. (1946). Science as a vocation. In H. H. Gerth, C. W. Mills (trans./eds.), *From Max Weber: Essays in sociology* (pp. 129–156). New York: Oxford University Press.